THE 12 DAYS

of

CHRISTMAS

THE 12 DAYS
of
CHRISTMAS

A Guide to an Old Tradition
with a New Purpose

Linda Coates & Leslie S. Kelly

Tate Publishing & Enterprises

⌒DEDICATION⌒

FROM LESLIE:

To Jesus, who makes everyday worth living. Thank you for rescuing me from the pit and blessing me beyond all comprehension.

To Don, who makes everyday worth loving. You are my best friend, and I am so blessed to be your wife. I definitely married "up". I honor and respect you with all that I am.

And to my children: Alicia, Sarah, Sam, Josiah, and Faith who make every day more interesting! You bring me such joy and I can't imagine how boring my life would be had I not been blessed with each one of you.

And to my dear friend and cohort in mischief, Linda: I am so thankful God brought us together and knit our hearts. Thank you for being a kindred spirit and for walking with me through thick and thin. I am so blessed to have you as my friend.

FROM LINDA:

To my God and my Lord and Savior, who, I am honored to serve.

To My Husband, Michael, who, I respect and admire greatly. Thank you for supporting me in this endeavor.

To my children: because without them I would not have been inspired to go on this adventure of writing a book. Amber-Rose, Brandon, Andrew & Sarah you have each been a blessing and a gift from God. I am so glad that God chose me to be your mom.

To my mom and dad who have always believed that I could do anything, and taught me to believe the same.

Lastly, to my friend, and sister in Christ, Leslie. God has greatly blessed me with our friendship. Without you, this book would have never been any more than a great personal journey and a new family tradition for a few close friends. Because of you many will enjoy a new blessing from God and a new way to celebrate.

TABLE OF CONTENTS

⌒⌒ FROM OUR HEARTS ⌒⌒

Ah, the holidays. We just love them. We love everything about them. Well, the positive things that is. We love the cool weather (I say cool, because in Florida, that's all you get) and for us, it means the end of the hurricane season, and the beginning of something special. We love the hustle and bustle, even though we sweat and fight traffic, (At least it is not in the snow!) and the baking and decorating. We especially love the times together as a family. But most of all, we love what this time of year means. Our Savior chose to come to earth as a baby, live without sin, and then sacrifice his life, so that we may live. Each Christmas, we try to savor every moment. We decorate, prepare meals, and try to do family devotionals for Advent. We don't want to miss anything the season has to offer. We want our children to understand that it is not about the gifts that we receive (and there always seem to be too many) but about the gift he gave. This is supposed to be about Christ, not us. Whose birthday is it anyway? But even with the best intentions, when all is said and done, we always feel a "let down." Like somehow in all the hustle and bustle, we missed it.

Face it; if you are like us, you lose focus with all the fuss over Christmas. We hate to admit that as Christians we get caught up in the "Holiday Rush," but we do. We are doing very well if we get through a small Advent devotional every other day or so. With recitals, plays, and parties, not to mention decorating, shopping, and baking, sometimes the Christ in Christmas gets shoved aside until we are sitting impatiently at the Christmas Eve service, wondering if we got everything done and where the season of peace and goodwill toward men has gone. We chide ourselves, promising next year will be different and confess our inadequacies to our Savior who is waiting with open arms, to love us in spite of our poor memory. And somehow, no matter how hard we try, the whirlwind sweeps us away again year after year. It's not that the activities aren't worthwhile or a blessing to others and to us. It just seems that so many things happen in such a short time that we are left feeling let down when it is all over. We plan and prepare and then, whoosh, in one fell swoop, it's over.

There is so much work and preparation for just one day. We felt like Christmas should be the jumping-off point, for the true celebration. We knew that things needed to change, but what? And how would we ever do it? We began to seek the Lord and he showed us that what we needed was a paradigm shift of Christmas; a change of focus.

God began working in both our hearts, giving us a deepening desire to reclaim the season. We yearned for more time to truly celebrate after the preparation. We wanted to give gifts to our Savior. We wanted Christmastime to be more about Christ and less about us, and we wanted our children to have this in their hearts, too.

We had been talking about how we could practically do this, and these things were in our heart one day when we were in a local wholesale club doing some Christmas shopping. We saw twelve stackable Christmas gift boxes, and it was as if God put the pieces together. It instantly hit us that instead of gifts to us, we are to give gifts back to him and the way we could do this was through stories and scriptures of *The Twelve Days of Christmas*. We knew that *The Twelve Days of Christmas* was more than the cute song that we sing at Christmas. However, we also knew that the meaning had been lost over the years, and that we needed not only to find what was lost, but also create a practical and interactive way to implement it into our lives while including all that God had placed on our hearts. We wrote down what he taught us, and the result is this guide.

During our research and prayer, God showed up and taught us that Christmas shouldn't be the end; it is just the beginning. The preparation for Christmas is necessary. We have family obligations and we desire to have a wonderful family day. But Christmas day is just the beginning of the true celebration. He also reminded us that the Jewish customs and celebrations were all given for teaching; to remind the old and teach the young the truths that were so important to them, and to God. That is what we hope this little book will be for you and your family; a new way to impart eternal truths through celebration, reflection, and refocus.

We would like to thank everyone who lovingly prayed us through this endeavor. It has been like being in labor and now we have finally given birth! We would also like to thank all the families who were our testers. Your comments were invaluable. We would especially like to thank Becca Puglisi, Amy Hillberg, Susan Golder and Ann Kite. Your help and comments were invaluable and we thank you from the bottom of our hearts. We would also like to thank the team at Tate Publishing: thank you for taking a chance on us and believing in our work even more than we did. You have been such a blessing. To our wonderful husbands Michael and Don: words cannot express our gratitude for the many times you fended for yourself for dinner, took care of things, and listened to our endless ramblings, we say "*I Love You*" and we owe you big time! Lastly, to our guinea pigs, aka, our children, Amber-Rose, Brandon, Andrew, Sarah, Alicia, Sarah, Sam, Josiah, and Faith, we say: thanks for your inspiration, patience, and for letting us experiment on you. See, we told you that we would put your names in print. Feels pretty good, doesn't it. And, *we are done!* Now we can start our next project!

For you, our fellow sojourners, our prayer is that you will truly enjoy the busyness of the season, and pour yourself into ministry to others at every precious opportunity God orchestrates for you. Let God use you, but don't leave him out. Serve from a heart full of him. Then when it's all over, as you give back to Christ through the Twelve Days, you will sense his spirit refreshing and refocusing your heart and your life. We hope you will find, as we have, that this is an awesome way to end the old year and begin the next. It is such an amazing way to celebrate the New Year. Not just one day, but twelve. We pray that you will use this and let God slow your heart, refresh your spirit, and restore your soul.

In Jesus,
Linda and Leslie

We thought you might like to have a little background information about *The Twelve Days of Christmas*. We also wanted you to know that as authors, we have taken liberties with these stories we have written. Most of them are fictional, written to help you understand and apply the concept of the day. A few of them are historical, and we have done our best to research and find out the truth and convey it honestly while still making it interesting. Others are from scripture, but embellished as we would imagine them. This was not done to change the meaning of the story, but to help you be able to place yourself in the story and try to understand what the characters would be feeling, seeing, and sensing as they lived out the situation they were in. It was done with lots of prayer, and careful thought to make it as meaningful and true to the scriptural basis as possible.

As we did research on the origins of the song; "Twelve Days of Christmas" and its meaning, we found that the history of the traditions surrounding the twelve days, as well as the origins of the song, are complicated and sketchy.

No one knows how the tradition got started, but it is known that the Twelfth Day is known as Three Kings Day, or Epiphany, (which means "to show, to make known or to reveal"). This is the day that we celebrate the Magi or Wise Men arriving to present gifts to the young Jesus, and by doing so, "reveal" him as Lord and King. Different churches and calendars date the twelfth night on January 6th or 7th, and the Eastern Orthodox Church celebrate it on January 19th because, in their calendar, Christmas falls on January 6th, also known as old Christmas.

Traditional English and French celebrations, which are held on January 5th, include feasting, taking down the Christmas decorations, and a King's Cake.

The song "The Twelve Days of Christmas" is the subject of debate. Some believe that during the religious wars of the 16th century, there were hidden meanings for each verse of the song, and that each verse teaches a basic tenant of the faith. It was written to pass down the truths of the faith from parents to children in a time when talking about them openly was a crime. It was a simple song with repeated verses so that children could easily learn their heritage. Others say that this is just a legend, and there were never any hidden meanings, and that it is just a silly song that is fun to sing. There is little evidence for either side.

It is certainly possible that the song is purely fun. But it is just as possible that the legend is factual. We do not want to take a solid stand; but rather take something that is well known, and already a part of our tradition and use it to celebrate our Christian faith and heritage as well as bring the focus back to our Savior. This is another avenue to the true meaning of Christmas. And perhaps, by the liberties we have taken as authors, the next time you or your children hear this nonsense song, it will remind you of God's grace and his transforming power in your life and in our world. If that happens, then our purpose has been accomplished.

⌐ HOW TO USE THIS BOOK ⌐

First, we want to thank you for taking this adventure with us. This whole project was God inspired, and he has shown up at every turn. This guide is meant to be user-friendly. You should start it on December 26th and finish on January 6th, which is Epiphany, or Three Kings Day. We hope you will end your journey with a Three Kings Party, also known as a Twelfth Night Feast. This party is a highlight of our celebration, and reinforces all we have done over the past twelve days.

If you celebrate Christmas with Advent candles, keep those out and light the Christ candle as you read the story and scripture each day. We really like doing this because it helps keep us focused on the reason for the twelve days as well as giving us the opportunity to use that big, beautiful candle that otherwise would have been discarded. (Here in Florida we can't put it in the attic—it would melt in the summer heat!)

We also suggest that you keep your decorations and Christmas tree up for the entire twelve days. It makes for great conversation when friends come over and ask, "Why is your tree still up?" It provides the perfect opportunity for your children to share what they are learning. And after all, you worked hard getting all those decorations put up, why not enjoy them for a few more days? Since our families have been doing this, we have actually been ready to put the decorations away on January 7th, unlike before, when we felt pressured to have them taken down and put away by the first or second of January.

Each child will need his own journal. He or she can use this year after year, and compare their spiritual growth from year to year. As an alternative to the hand written journal, you could set up a blog for your child on a blog site. There are several safe and enjoyable blog sites on the internet that are available to use. Whichever method you choose to log your journey, be sure to encourage your children to do it by setting the example. We also encourage you to take pictures and add those to your journal also. Or you could do a scrapbook if you are so inclined.

A word about the suggested ornaments: we are in the process of locating a supplier for ornaments you may purchase. We will keep you updated on our website, www.12daysbook.com, so be sure to check it frequently. We also have several suggestions for making them. One suggestion is to reduce the coloring pages and decorate them to put on your tree or a wall. You could also make them out of polymer clay, which you must bake, or you could use air dry clay. Whatever you choose to make, email pictures to us and we will post them on our website. We would love to see your work. (Isn't technology wonderful?)

Each day is divided into 12 sections. The first nine, Song, Symbolism, Verse, Concept, Story, Discussion Questions, Points to Ponder, Gift and Prayer, are the crucial elements. They will take you about 15–20 minutes to complete. If you have older children, you may especially enjoy the Points to Ponder. We created this section to help inspire deeper conversation, and strengthen their faith. We want them to be able to think for themselves and help them have a deep, abiding love for Christ Jesus. This discussion may take significantly more than 15 minutes, but it will be so worthwhile. The last three, Suggested Activities, Bringing it Home to your Heart, and Be His Hands and Feet, could take significantly longer. We suggest you read through these sections before beginning, so you can be prepared ahead of time. We included a Preparation Guide to assist you with this. Every activity is listed in order of the days so you can familiarize yourself with what you will need to have on hand or do in advance as preparation for that day. Also, on our website www.12daysbook.com you will find many of the links and resources we mention throughout this guide. Hopefully, this will take some of the frustration out of your preparation.

As you begin each day, sing "The Twelve Days of Christmas" up to the day you are on. A copy of the lyrics can be found prior to the daily guides. The written music is in Appendix B.

We strongly encourage you to choose some memory verses from the ones listed in Appendix A to memorize during this journey. It is so important that your children keep God's Word in their hearts, and it is great for them to copy them in their journal as well. They will be blessed by doing this, and not just now, but in their adult lives as well.

One final note: we have taken the liberty of paraphrasing and embellishing some of the Bible stories in these pages. We have added feeling and emotion and tried to take the reader into the story. Every attempt was made to keep it authentic and to the point. This was only done in the stories. The scripture verses are as they are found in the New International Version of the Bible. If you prefer another translation, feel free to use it.

Again, we thank you for using this guide. Please visit us at our website, www.12daysbook.com and let us know how you used it, and what you learned. We pray God's richest blessings on your family as you seek to honor him through *The Twelve Days of Christmas* and throughout the New Year.

PREPARATION GUIDE

The Twelve Days of Christmas is a study guide meant to help you focus on Christ during this busy season. It's filled with fun and challenging activities and outings for a wide spectrum of ages. It's an ideal study to share with another family, small group, or home-school group. We had great fun doing this and our kids enjoyed completing the activities together.

To fully experience *The Twelve Days of Christmas,* some advanced preparation is necessary. This *Preparation Guide* will make the experience less stressful for you and more fun and meaningful for your children.

Before you begin, browse each day's *Suggested Activities* and decide which ones will be appropriate for your family. Then use the preparation guide to identify the items you will need. This shouldn't be too difficult. Many of the materials you may already have on hand, especially if you like to bake during the holidays.

In some of the lessons, you will find more activities than you could possibly complete. The purpose of this is to give you options. If an activity looks too difficult or doesn't fit your needs, skip it. Choose the ones that are right for you or implement your own ideas. If you come up with something innovative and exciting, please let us know. We would love to hear from you!

A note about suggested outings: if you try to do them all, you'll be running on empty by the end of the study. Many different ideas were included so you can repeat this lesson plan each year and keep it fresh and meaningful for your families.

SUGGESTED OUTINGS

Day 1: a trip to a homeless shelter, nursing home, or children's home or hospital. Visitation policies vary, so be sure to contact the facility in advance about volunteering. If you'd like to bring goodies, find out what is allowed and how many you should bring.

Day 5: a visit to a synagogue. This outing is a great opportunity for children to learn about their roots and will likely spark meaningful spiritual discussions among family members.

Day 7: doing free chores or yard work for someone in need, like an elderly person, widow, neighbor, or friend. They will likely offer you payment for your services, but remember that your work is your gift to them. Be sure to take that into consideration as you set up this appointment.

Day 8: volunteering at a local soup kitchen. Many of these facilities receive an abundance of volunteers during the holidays. If you would like to participate, call well in advance. If you cannot physically serve at the facility, ask if you can donate food or prepare dessert for a meal. You can also help kitchens that host a public food pantry by donating items.

Day 9: a trip to the ballet to see *The Nutcracker.* Many theatres offer a matinee or school show early in December. Reserve your tickets in advance. If attending the ballet is not a possibility, we suggest renting *The Nutcracker* performance starring Mikhael Baryshnikov. This older version may be difficult to find, but it is well worth the effort.

Day 10: visiting a local government building where the Ten Commandments are posted. You can usually find such a building at your local courthouse or county seat. Call ahead of time to find out when they are open to the public.

Day 12: host a Three Kings party. You will find a party guide in Appendix A for potential games and ideas. Make this your own unique event, but remember to include a time for the children to share what they have learned and how it has affected their lives. Use this party to celebrate the idea of following Christ into the New Year. Also celebrate his gifts of family, friends, and faith today and every day of the year to come.

⟵ SUPPLY LIST ⟶

DAILY SUPPLIES

- Journal for each participant
- Pens/pencils
- Bible
- An ornament to represent each of the twelve days of Christmas
- Print the gift scrolls to place in the boxes or gift bags. You can print them on beautiful Christmas paper directly from our website www.12daysbook.com or you can find them in Appendix B.
- Copy the coloring pages, one for each child who would enjoy using them. There are 12, one for each day and are located in Appendix B, or you can print them directly from our website.
- Boxes or gift bags to hold each day's supplies
- Crayons, markers, colored pencils, and watercolor paints and brushes (for older children)

You might also like to include a disposable camera for each person, to create a photo journal of the experience.

If you use an advent wreath, light the center candle as you read the entry for each day. This way, you will get more use out of that big, beautiful candle.

SUPPLIES FOR INDIVIDUAL LESSONS

Day 1: Ingredients for "goodies" to take on your outing.

Day 2: Materials needed to make a birdfeeder (Appendix B).

Day 3: A dictionary, card-making supplies or store-bought cards, envelopes, and stamps.

Day 5: A copy of *The Golden Rule* for each child, one copy of *The Five Golden Rings of Obedience* per family (both in Appendix B), and Bundt cake ingredients (Appendix B).

Day 7: Spiritual Gift survey link, letter-writing materials, envelopes, stamps, and a soldier's address. Websites are listed in Appendix C.

Day 9: Sparkling grape juice or a fruit basket, a copy of *The Nutcracker* to watch (if going to the ballet is impossible), and items to make an encouragement card(s).

Day 10: A copy of *The Ten Commandments* (Appendix B) for each child, materials to make the Ten Commandments scroll and door plaque (Appendix B), letter-writing materials, envelopes, stamps, and a list of governing officials in your area (Appendix C).

Day 12: Ingredients for the "Three Kings Cake" (Appendix B), as well as necessary items for the party.

It is our sincere hope and prayer that *The Twelve Days of Christmas* will become a meaningful tradition in your family. Please contact us on our website www.12daysbook.com or directly at info@12daysbook.com and share your experiences with us. We look forward to hearing from you!

Day 1: Partridge in a pear tree
Verse: John 3:16
Represents: Jesus dying on the cross to save us from our sins

Day 2: Two turtle doves
Verse: Luke 2:22–24
Represents: The Old and New Testaments

Day 3: Three French hens
Verse: 1 Corinthians 13:13
Represents: The three virtues of faith, hope and love

Day 4: Four calling birds
Verse: John 20:31
Represents: The four gospels: Matthew, Mark, Luke and John

Day 5: Five golden rings
Verse: Psalm 19:9–10
Represents: The Torah, which are the Books of Moses, the Law

Day 6: Six geese-a-laying
Verse: Genesis 1:1
Represents: New life, and the six days of creation

Day 7: Seven swans-a-swimming
Verse: Romans 12:6–8
Represents: The seven gifts of the Holy Spirit

Day 8: Eight maids-a-milking
Verse: Matthew 5:3–10
Represents: The eight Beatitudes

Day 9: Nine ladies dancing
Verse: Galatians 5:22–23
Represents: The fruit of the Spirit

Day 10: Ten lords-a-leaping
Verse: Exodus 20:2–17
Represents: The Ten Commandments

Day 11: Eleven pipers piping
Verse: Mark 3:16–19
Represents: The 11 faithful disciples

Day 12: Twelve drummers drumming
Verse: *The Apostles Creed*
Represents: The 12 tenants of our faith

⟵ THE LYRICS ⟶

"THE TWELVE DAYS OF CHRISTMAS"

On the first day of Christmas my true love gave to me: a partridge in a pear tree.

On the second day of Christmas my true love gave to me: two turtle doves, and a partridge in a pear tree.

On the third day of Christmas my true love gave to me: three French hens, two turtle doves, and a partridge in a pear tree.

On the fourth day of Christmas my true love gave to me: four calling birds, three French hens, two turtle doves, and a partridge in a pear tree.

On the fifth day of Christmas my true love gave to me: five golden rings, four calling birds, three French hens, two turtle doves, and a partridge in a pear tree.

On the sixth day of Christmas my true love gave to me: six geese a laying, five golden rings, four calling birds, three French hens, two turtle doves, and a partridge in a pear tree.

On the seventh day of Christmas my true love gave to me: seven swans a swimming, six geese a laying, five golden rings, four calling birds, three French hens, two turtle doves, and a partridge in a pear tree.

On the eighth day of Christmas my true love gave to me: eight maids a milking, seven swans a swimming, six geese a laying, five golden rings, four calling birds, three French hens, two turtle doves, and a partridge in a pear tree.

On the ninth day of Christmas my true love gave to me: nine ladies dancing, eight maids a milking, seven swans a swimming, six geese a laying, five golden rings, four calling birds, three French hens, two turtle doves, and a partridge in a pear tree.

On the tenth day of Christmas my true love gave to me: ten lords a leaping, nine ladies dancing, eight maids a milking, seven swans a swimming, six geese a laying, five golden rings, four calling birds, three French hens, two turtle doves, and a partridge in a pear tree.

On the eleventh day of Christmas my true love gave to me: eleven pipers piping, ten lords a leaping, nine ladies dancing, eight maids a milking, seven swans a swimming, six geese a laying, five golden rings, four calling birds, three French hens, two turtle doves, and a partridge in a pear tree.

On the twelfth day of Christmas my true love gave to me: twelve drummers drumming, eleven pipers piping, ten lords a leaping, nine ladies dancing, eight maids a milking, seven swans a swimming, six geese a laying, five golden rings, four calling birds, three French hens, two turtle doves, and a partridge in a pear tree.

The link to the sheet music http://christmassongbook.net/s12_days.asp

⤙ THE FIRST DAY OF CHRISTMAS ⤚

On the first day of Christmas, my true love gave to me…
a partridge in a pear tree.

DAY 1, DECEMBER 26

SYMBOLISM

The partridge: Jesus, who gave his life for us
The pear tree: The cross, the tree upon which he was crucified
My true love: God, the one who loves us enough to give us his only Son

VERSE

For God so loved the world that he gave his one and only Son, that whoever believes in him shall not perish but have eternal life. (John 3:16)

CONCEPT

God's first and best gift to us was Jesus Christ, his Son.

TODAY'S STORY

I once heard a story about a firefighter in California who took a walk through the ravaged forest after a fire. As he took in the sight of such loss and devastation he came across what appeared to be a charred rock. Upon closer inspection, he realized that it was a small bird, a partridge, which had chosen to stay down on the ground, spread its wings, and die. The firefighter was disturbed by this, knowing that the partridge could have flown away to safety. In his frustration at such a meaningless death, he kicked the ashen, petrified bird. At that moment from underneath the ashes, scurried out several baby chicks. This was not a meaningless death; the mother partridge had sacrificed her life willingly to save her children from certain death. It was a price she readily paid. This is a beautiful picture of what Christ did for us. He covered us with his love and sacrificed *himself* so that we might live.

DISCUSSION QUESTIONS

1. Who loves you the most?
    God the father

2. What is the greatest and best gift God has given to you?
    His Son, Jesus Christ

3. Why did he give his Son for you?
    So I could have eternal life

4. Since he gave his life for you, what can you give to him?
    My life and my all

POINTS TO PONDER

Understand sacrifice and what it means. For example: parents sacrifice their time, money, and energy to raise their children well. We can sacrifice with a joyful heart or out of obligation. Which one of these, joy or obligation, do you think will be a blessing? We need to truly comprehend what sacrifice is in order to appreciate what Jesus has done for us.

GIFT

God gave us the first and best gift, which was his Son, Jesus Christ. Our first gift to him should be ourselves. Dedicate your life to him afresh and ask Jesus to help you finish this year and start the next with him as your guide.

PRAYER

Dear Lord Jesus, thank you for this year that is drawing to a close. Thank you for the gifts you've given us and for the hope of the year to come. As we anticipate this new beginning, guide our hearts, minds, and actions so that we can be more like you and reflect your glory. May we always praise you for your power and glory. In Jesus' name, amen.

SUGGESTED ACTIVITIES

OPEN THE FIRST GIFT BOX AND HANG THE PARTRIDGE ORNAMENT ON YOUR TREE.

BRINGING IT HOME TO YOUR HEART

We suggest that if you have not done so, go through the memory verses listed in Appendix A. Choose the ones you think are appropriate for the ages and stages of your children, and begin memorizing them on the appropriate days. For today, copy the chosen verse in your journal and write your prayer of commitment for the upcoming year. Help younger children understand the meaning of commitment. Allow them to draw pictures of what it means to them and how they will respond.

BE HIS HANDS AND FEET

Take an afternoon trip to see how we can shelter those who cannot shelter themselves. Spread some of his joy by visiting a homeless shelter, a children's home, a nursing home, a hospital, or another place of your choosing. If the facilities allow it, bring along some goodies to share. These could be candy, home-baked cookies or just a song and a smile.

⟿ THE SECOND DAY OF CHRISTMAS ⟿

On the second day of Christmas, my true love gave to me...
two turtledoves.

DAY 2, DECEMBER 27

SYMBOLISM

The *two turtledoves* represent the Old and New Testaments of the Bible, which are God's love story to us. Jesus is the fulfillment of the Old Testament prophesies.

VERSE

When the time of their purification according to the Law of Moses had been completed, Joseph and Mary took him to Jerusalem to present him to the Lord, (as it is written in the Law of the Lord, "Every firstborn male is to be consecrated to the Lord") and to offer a sacrifice in keeping with what is said in the Law of the Lord: "a pair of doves or two young pigeons." (Luke 2:22–24)

CONCEPT

Jesus Christ is the fulfillment of the Old Testament prophesies.

TODAY'S STORY

The turtledove is a beautiful and innocent bird. It is mentioned frequently in the Bible, where it was often used as a sacrifice to God as atonement for sins. In fact, Mary and Joseph brought two turtledoves to the temple as a sacrifice for their newborn son, baby Jesus.

King David referenced the dove in the 55th Psalm when he said, "Oh that I had wings like a dove! For then I would flee away and be at rest. Lo, then would

I wander far off and remain in the wilderness. I would hasten my escape from the windy storm and tempest."

Doves are interesting creatures. They will nest just about anywhere they feel safe, even if it is on a craggy, mountain face or, as in Biblical times, among the ash pots on the rooftops and porches of houses. These pots were used to store ashes from the fires people lit to keep warm at night. The doves would nest in and around the pots for warmth and safety. When they took flight from these dusty perches, the birds were often covered in soot. But as soon as they took to the air, the dust and ash would fling off and they would be as beautiful as ever. I think that may have been what David saw when he penned that verse. When you think about it, that is what Christ has done for us. We were living among the ash pots, dirty with sin and selfishness. When he came into our lives, he flung off our sin, and made us white as snow.

The second day of Christmas is harkened by two turtledoves, representing the Old and the New Testaments. The Old Testament foretells the coming of the Messiah, the one who would not abolish the law, but fulfill it. The New Testament tells of Messiah's coming and his once-and-for-all atonement of our sin. Together, they bear witness to his story, the history of God's deep and abiding love for people, and the price he was willing to pay to bring those that he loved into his grace.

DISCUSSION QUESTIONS:

1. Traditionally what do doves symbolize?
    Love, purity and peace.

2. In today's story what do doves symbolize?
    The Old and New Testaments, God's love letter to us.

3. What gift did God use to allow us to better understand him and his love for us?
    The Bible, the Old and New Testament. They point to Christ as the fulfillment of Old Testament prophecy by coming to earth to be a servant King that many would reject.

4. Since he gave this gift for you, what can you do with it?
    Plant God's Word deep in our hearts so it can take root and grow. Memorize the books of the Bible.

POINTS TO PONDER

Another point of discussion is the fact that, as Christians, we were grafted into the root of Judah, just like a grape vine can be grafted into a well established root. This means that we as believers, not from the line of Abraham, can share in the same blessings and inheritance as his descendants. Discuss what that means to you.

GIFT

God gave us a precious gift, the Bible, as a love letter in the form of the Old and New Testaments. This is how we can know him and his direction for our lives. Our gift to him is to get to know him through his very special book.

PRAYER

Dear Lord Jesus, thank you for the Bible, which is your Word, and what you have taught us through it. Thank you that you revealed your heart and your love for us through both the Old and New Testaments. May we honor you this year, by hiding your Word in our hearts so that we might not sin against you. May we be children who hear and obey. In Jesus' name, amen.

SUGGESTED ACTIVITIES

OPEN THE SECOND GIFT BOX AND PLACE THE TWO TURTLEDOVES ORNAMENT ON YOUR TREE.

BRINGING IT HOME TO YOUR HEART

Work on your memory verse by playing the Bounce Back game (Appendix A). If you do not know them, this year may be a good time to try to memorize the books of the Bible. An easy way to learn these is a song recorded by Wee Sing. Record in your journal why it is important to write God's Word on your heart. Play the Prophecy Matching Game or the Obedience Game, or conduct a Bible drill. Rules for the games are listed in Appendix A.

Listen to this beautiful white dove cooing.
http://www.youtube.com/watch?v=8q7Zz39RBak& NR=1

BE HIS HANDS AND FEET

Purchase or make a bird feeder (Appendix B). Give it to your pastor or someone who is influential in your spiritual growth. Attach a note of thanks for their faithful service to you. You could also begin a prayer journal to remind you to pray for others and keep a log of God's answers.

～THE THIRD DAY OF CHRISTMAS～

On the third day of Christmas, my true love gave to me...
three French hens.

DAY 3, DECEMBER 28

SYMBOLISM

The *three French hens* represent the three gifts of the Magi: Frankincense, Gold, and Myrrh, which are the virtues of faith, hope, and love.

VERSE

And now these three remain: faith, hope and love. But the greatest of these is love. (1 Corinthians 13:13)

CONCEPT

God has given his followers the unrivaled treasures of faith, hope, and love. We must choose to live by them.

TODAY'S STORY

In the Bible, there is a story about a widow. She had no husband, no children and no means to make an income. She had nothing left. Yet, that day, she chose to go to the temple. Jesus was there. He knew her: her quiet life, her meager means. As she quietly approached the offering box, she was pushed out of the way by a wealthy temple official. He was dressed in fine silk and linen and carried a large, bulging purse. He sauntered up to the offering box, pushing others aside, and in his most pompous voice, he made sure everyone within earshot heard the auspicious amount that he was giving. People gasped. The huge amount was roughly what the temple might receive in a whole year! As he strolled off, so proud of himself and his gift, many people patted his back and shook his hand. But Jesus was not impressed. He could see past the man's fancy clothes and trimmings straight to his heart, and Jesus knew that because of all his money, there was no room for him there.

Meanwhile, the widow finally reached the offering box. After that ostentatious display, she just wanted to give her money and be on her way. She was almost embarrassed for the man, and at her small, insignificant offering. But it was all she had, and she had worked hard for it, so she meekly dropped her two coins in the box with great joy.

The people around Jesus began to murmur, and he asked: "Who do you think gave the greatest gift?" They all began discussing it among themselves. Of course it was the rich man! He gave an enormous amount of money that would be used to do many good things. The widow's money wouldn't even buy a loaf of bread for the poor. Why did she even bother?

But Jesus quieted the crowd, and then shocked them with his answer. It was not the rich man who had given the greatest gift, but the widow. The wealthy official gave out of his plenty, from an empty heart that just wanted to impress everyone. But the widow gave all that she had, from a heart full of faith, hope, and love.

Her gift was the most precious, as is ours when we give it from the heart. For you see, God doesn't want your money until he has you. Then he provides you with gifts that you can give back to him. It says in the Bible that without faith, it is impossible to please God. That is step one. We must have faith in him. Faith leads to hope, which no one can take away from us. It is another of God's gifts. And with faith and hope, we can see people as he sees them, and truly love them.

I imagine the widow felt sorry for the rich man, for her heart was full and she could see that his was empty. How sad, that the rich man went away with a full purse but an empty heart. No faith, no hope, and no real love. The widow's story ended quite the opposite: she went away empty handed, but with a full heart, having had the privilege not only to see Jesus, but also to experience his love firsthand.

DISCUSSION QUESTIONS

1. Who loved God more, the widow or the rich man?
    The widow

2. Why was her gift so significant?
    Because it was all she had and it came from her heart

3. What gift does Jesus want from you?
    All of me…time, money, and talents.

4. What gift would be a sacrifice for you to give? Are you willing to give it?
    Answers will vary

POINTS TO PONDER

Another point for discussion is Matthew 6:2 "So when you give to the needy, do not announce it with trumpets, as the hypocrites do in the synagogues and on the streets, to be honored by men. I tell you the truth; they have received their reward in full."

Discuss the motivation behind your gifts and where you will receive your reward. Another great story of sacrificial giving you might want to read is 1 Kings 17 (Elijah and the widow).

One of the things we found while doing our research was a great website that melds the history and legend of the three wise men. It was very interesting and we thought you might like to take a look too. It gives a description of each of the wise men and their gifts as well as what they represent. Here is a brief description of the Magi and what they brought to the King. This is based on history and legend but is still interesting. For further information here is a link.

http://www.hymnsandcarolsofchristmas.com/Text/concerning_the_magi_and_their_na.htm

Gold was given by *Melchoir*. He was the oldest of the Magi, and had a long, grey beard. As the King of Arabia he understood the royal implications of his gift. The gold symbolized his *faith* in *Christ's Kingship*.

Frankincense was given by *Balthazar*. He was a dark-complexioned man with a beard, the King of Ethiopia. Frankincense is an incense used at prayer, it is a symbol of divinity, our *hope* in Christ. Frankincense symbolized Christ as *High Priest*.

Myrrh was given by *Caspar*. He was the youngest, said to be in his twenties. Myrrh was used as a perfume used in preparing bodies for burial and as a medicine. Myrrh symbolized Christ's *love* for us as the *Healer and Great Physician*.

GIFT

Since God gave us these three gifts, faith, hope and love, we should give them back to him by having faith and hope in him, and loving him with our whole hearts. We should also give these gifts back to him to use in us, so that we may be able to truly show love to people. Ask him to grow these qualities in your life so that you may be an example to others.

PRAYER

Heavenly Father, thank you for your wonderful gifts. I love you so much. I pray that you will increase my faith as I give myself to you. I put my hope in you. You know what is best for me and I know you will meet my needs because you love me. Thank you so much. In Jesus' name, amen.

SUGGESTED ACTIVITIES

OPEN THE THIRD GIFT BOX AND PLACE THE THREE FRENCH HENS ORNAMENT ON YOUR TREE.

BRINGING IT HOME TO YOUR HEART

Look up the definitions of faith, hope, and love in a dictionary. Compare the information to what the Bible has to say about these three virtues. Look up verses in your concordance and definitions in a Bible dictionary, if you have one. Discuss and create your best definition for each. Write them in your journal, along with where the verses are found. You could also start a list of your favorite verses. Read 1 Corinthians 13 to gain a better understanding of today's key verse. Review books of the Bible and memory verse.

BE HIS HANDS AND FEET

God has given us the gifts of faith, hope, and love. Share these gifts by sending a card to someone who needs encouragement, like a shut-in, someone who has suffered loss, or a person struggling with illness. Also, consider supporting a child through a world help organization like Compassion International, World Vision, Samaritan's Purse, or another worthy group. The contact information for these groups is listed in Appendix C.

PREPARATION

Materials
- Daily supplies
- four calling birds ornament for day four
- Scroll

Before You Start

Fill the gift box or bag with the day's materials.

~ THE FOURTH DAY OF CHRISTMAS ~

On the fourth day of Christmas, my true love gave to me…
four calling birds.

DAY 4, DECEMBER 29

SYMBOLISM

The *four calling birds* represent the four gospels: Matthew, Mark, Luke, and John, which tell us the good news of God sending Jesus to reconcile us to himself.

VERSE

But these are written that you may believe that Jesus is the Christ, the Son of God, and that by believing you may have life in his name. (John 20:31)

CONCEPT

The four gospels: Mathew, Mark, Luke, and John, all tell the story of Jesus.
Each sing the same song but have a different tune. We, too, have a song to sing.

TODAY'S STORY

One day a prince was out walking in a forest. All was calm and quiet with the exception of a few faint rustling sounds here and there in the trees. As he walked, he was captivated by the peacefulness that surrounded him. He came upon a small clearing and noticed that a tree had fallen. He thought this would be a perfect spot to stop and rest. It was so peaceful that he almost fell asleep.

Suddenly, his peace was shattered by a bird that started to sing. At first it sang alone, but soon another bird joined in, then a third and a fourth, all singing their own songs. The prince was annoyed. Their songs sounded like noisy competition to him. He covered his ears and tried to clear his head. When he took his hands away, he was shocked to find that the noisy bird voices had settled into a glorious four-part harmony. It was the most beautiful sound he had ever heard, better than the music produced by the most skilled musicians in the kingdom.

So it is with the four gospels. Matthew, Mark, Luke, and John all tell the story of Christ's love for us. Some say they contradict each other, but they do not. Each writer tells the Greatest Story from his own perspective and together, they form a harmonious union. So it is with us; each one of us has a different personality, with different points of view, which gives us our own story to tell. The four gospels were written so that whatever our circumstance, we can relate to God's message of love and forgiveness to us through his son, Jesus, and be able to share our story with others.

DISCUSSION QUESTIONS

1. What does the gospel mean to you?
    Answers will vary, but, it is the story of Christ and His love for us.

2. Which of the four gospels is your favorite?
    Answers will vary

3. What do you think God wants us to do with the four gospels that he sent us?
    Know them and understand them so that we can share our own story with others.

POINTS TO PONDER

Discuss the perspective of the four gospels. The Stories are not identical because they were all written by different people experiencing different things. Here is a little bit about each of the four disciples to help you understand a bit more about them and their vantage point.

Matthew: A Jewish tax collector. He links the Old Testament to the New Testament with the emphasis on Jesus the Messiah as the fulfillment of Old Testament prophecy.

Mark: He was not one of the original twelve, but he accompanied Paul on his first missionary journey. His account is chronological and records more miracles than the other Gospels. It is also the shortest.

Luke: A doctor and the only gentile. He gives the most comprehensive and accurate account of Christ's life. Luke was one of the very first Christians.

John: A fisherman, son of Zebedee, and the brother of James. He proves conclusively that Jesus was and is the heaven-sent Son of God and the only source of life. He gives a powerful argument for the incarnation of Christ.

GIFT

God gave us the gift of the four gospels. As your gift to him, take the time this year to read though the four gospels. Learn their stories and how they complement each other. Also note the differences. Understand that each writer had his own personality and saw Jesus in a different light. This gives us a deeper and richer account of his life. Just like when a report is given of a particular event, the more people who tell the story, the broader the perspective. Knowing and understanding God's Word is not only a gift to God, but also a gift he gives to us.

PRAYER

Father, thank you for giving us four different views of your Son. Thank you that you meet us wherever we are and however you made us. We are grateful that you love us so much. May we honor you by getting to know your Word better. In Jesus' name, amen.

SUGGESTED ACTIVITIES

OPEN THE FOURTH GIFT BOX AND PLACE THE FOUR CALLING BIRDS ORNAMENT ON YOUR TREE.

BRINGING IT HOME TO YOUR HEART

The gospels tell us Jesus' story. But what about your own? Your story is called your testimony. It is unique to you, because it is what God has done in your life as you've learned how to trust him. Begin to record your story in your journal by writing one thing that is special to you about Jesus—one way that he is unique to your needs. You could also find a verse in one of the four gospels that is special to you and record that, too. Don't forget to review your memory verse.

BE HIS HANDS AND FEET

Tell someone your story. It could be your mom or dad, brother or sister, or another trusted friend. The more you practice sharing your faith, the easier it becomes. Then you will be ready when God gives you the opportunity to share your story, and his, with others.

⁓ THE FIFTH DAY OF CHRISTMAS ⁓

On the fifth day of Christmas, my true love gave to me...
five golden rings.

DAY 5, DECEMBER 30

SYMBOLISM

The *five golden rings* represent the five books of Moses, known as the Torah, which is the law: Genesis, Exodus, Leviticus, Numbers, and Deuteronomy.

VERSE

The fear of the LORD is pure, enduring forever. The ordinances of the LORD are sure and altogether righteous. They are more precious than gold, than much pure gold; they are sweeter than honey, than honey from the comb. (Psalms 19:9–10)

CONCEPT

God's laws were written for our benefit. This is the foundation of our understanding of God. We need to study these books and trust God's wisdom. They are the promise of what is yet to come.

TODAY'S STORY

Did you know that the five golden rings of today's verse speak of yet another bird? It is the ring-necked pheasant. An ordinary pheasant has simple white rings around its neck, but the rink-necked pheasant is different. Its rings are golden; precious, shiny, dense, beautiful, golden rings.

Have you ever wondered why gold is so sought after? Here are a few of the things that make it so valuable and precious.

- People of the middle ages believed that gold was a source of immortality, so it was used in many medicines. Alchemists tried to use magic to make this precious metal.

- It is the most malleable metal known; a single ounce can be beaten into a 300 square- foot sheet of gold leaf, or spun into gold thread.

- Unlike other metals, gold is resistant to moisture, oxygen, heat, and most corrosive agents. This makes it suitable for use in jewelry, coins, and in electronic devices, since it does not corrode or tarnish.

- The standard touchtone phone would not function without the thirty-three contacts it contains that are made from gold.

- Air bag systems in more than thirty million cars around the world rely on gold-coated, electrical contacts to function properly.

- Every time you touch a key on your computer, it strikes a gold circuit that relays your command to the computer's microprocessor.

Gold has been a symbol for royalty, purity, wealth, and prestige. From what the Bible says, we know that Abraham was rich in gold and silver, and that Moses covered the mercy seat of the Ark of the Covenant with pure gold. Most of the gold ever mined is still in existence because it remains unaffected by the passage of time.

The same is true for the Torah, the five books of Moses. They haven't changed since the time they were written, and they're just as valuable now as they were then. In these books, God communicated his love and laws for his people, the Israelites. The Torah was more precious than gold to the children of Israel. In fact, King David wrote a Psalm to laud the perfection of these five books. In it, he said that:

1. *The Instruction of Adonai* is sure, trustworthy, God's wisdom.

2. *The Precepts of Adonai* are right, rejoicing the hearts.

3. *The Commands (Mitzvah) of Adonai* are pure, enlightening the eyes.

4. *The fear of Adonai* is clean, enduring forever.

5. *The Rulings of Adonai* are true, righteous, and altogether more desirable than gold.

It was true for the children of Israel, and it is true for us today.

DISCUSSION QUESTIONS

1. What are the similarities between gold and the laws of Moses?
    They are both valuable, long lasting, unaffected by time, and pure.

2. What does this mean for you?
    We need to appreciate the value of the Torah and rejoice because it is more precious than gold.

3. How can you know how to obey God's laws?
    Read and study the five books of Moses.

POINTS TO PONDER

Discuss the ways in which Jesus came to fulfill the requirements of the law (Five books of Moses) not to abolish it. Some other notable things are: a ring is eternal, never ending, stretched out over time, and all of mankind, as are the five books of Moses.

GIFT

God has given us so much, including the Torah. The best way to show him our gratitude is to hold these truths dear to our hearts, love his law, and try to be obedient to him.

PRAYER

Thank you, God, for the law that you gave us through our servant Moses. Help us to always see that it was given to us for our protection and to enlighten our hearts. May we learn true obedience and always hold your commands dear. In Jesus' name, amen.

SUGGESTED ACTIVITIES

OPEN THE FIFTH GIFT BOX AND PLACE THE FIVE GOLDEN RINGS ORNAMENT ON YOUR TREE.

BRINGING IT HOME TO YOUR HEART

Copy *The Golden Rule* (Appendix B) on a piece of construction paper, cardstock, or other decorative paper and in your journal. Decorate the pages however you choose. You might like to use markers, crayons, colored pencils or stickers.

Memorize "The Five Golden Rules of Obedience" (Appendix B). You can also decorate it and hang it some place where you will see it often and be reminded of what you learned. Record them in your journal. If possible, visit a synagogue. Ask the Rabbi to show you the Torah. Many still have it written in the form of a large beautiful scroll. If you ask, the Rabbi might even read some of it for you in the original Hebrew language. Don't forget to review your memory verse or begin to learn a new one.

BE HIS HANDS AND FEET

Bake a golden Bundt cake (Appendix B) or five mini-Bundt cakes. Share them with a neighbor or a friend and tell them what you have learned about gold and God's precious laws. You could even share your cake with the Rabbi at the synagogue. Just make sure the ingredients are kosher.

THE SIXTH DAY OF CHRISTMAS

On the sixth day of Christmas, my true love gave to me…
six geese-a-laying.

DAY 6, DECEMBER 31

SYMBOLISM

The *six geese-a-laying* represent new life, the new life created on the six days of creation.

VERSE

In the beginning, God created the heavens and the earth. (Genesis 1:1)

CONCEPT

God created the world in six days. On the seventh day, he rested. We need to marvel at the wonder of the design of this extraordinary world by keeping the Sabbath holy.

TODAY'S STORY

Creation…the beginning of life. That's what the geese-a-laying represent, new life. Why Six? Because the Bible says that God created the world in six days and on the seventh, he rested.

Have you ever wondered how the world was made? I mean, how it really happened? I believe it is a question that people have been trying to answer since the beginning of time. The Bible says that God created the heavens and the earth like this:

On the first day of creation he separated the light from darkness. God called the light "day," and the darkness he called "night."

On day two, God made the expanse, and separated the waters that were below, from the waters which were above. God called the expanse heaven.

On the third day, God called the dry ground "land," and caused the land to produce vegetation.

On day four, God made the two great lights, the greater light to govern the day, and the lesser light to govern the night; He made the stars also.

On the fifth day, He made the water teem with living creatures, and let birds fly above the earth across the expanse of the sky.

On the sixth day he said, let the earth bring forth living creatures after their kind: cattle and creeping things and beasts of the earth. God created man, male and female.

Then he rested on the seventh day from all his work.

Now that we have looked at what the Bible has to say, let's see what science tells us. We know from experience that accidents by nature can destroy. You name it: earthquakes, hurricanes, tornados, even car accidents. That is why they are called disasters and accidents. We may learn from them, but on their own they never create. A building needs a builder. A painting needs a painter. A creation needs a creator. If my son, (who would love to have the chance to safely blow something up) blew up an electronics store, would a computer form itself out of the disaster? Of course not. All the pieces are present to make a computer, but you must have an intelligent designer to do so. The scientist who wrote the forward to the 100 year anniversary edition of Darwin's *Origin of Species,* Sir Arthur Keith (1866–1955) said "Evolution is unproved and unprovable. We only believe it because the alternative is special creation, and that is unthinkable." What he is saying here is: the only reason they believe in evolution is because they don't want to believe in God.

Our planet has a moon, and it orbits around the sun, which is at the center of our solar system. Our solar system is found in the Milky Way which is only one of the billion galaxies in the universe. If any one of these pieces were a slightly different size or in a slightly different location, life could not exist. I am often amazed at the incredible vastness and wonder of nature. For me, it points to one conclusion: intelligent design.

Our body, for example, is made up of trillions of cells. Each cell is made from approximately 60,000 proteins. A single protein has about 400 amino acids. Even the simplest life form is not so simple. Now let's look at one of those tiny little proteins. It is made up of 124 amino acids all lined up in perfect order. The chances of them lining up in this perfect order all by themselves are 1 in 10 to the power of 152. Just what does that mean?

Here's another way to imagine it: let's say six friends are standing side by side for you to take their picture, but you can't decide what order you would like to place them. If you arranged your friends into every possible order and took one picture every minute, how long do you think it would it take you? Here is how you do it. You multiply 1x2x3x4x5x6. That would be 720 minutes which equals 12 hours!

Imagine if you had 18 friends to arrange? That would be over six quadrillion possibilities and would take over twelve billion years! I don't even want to do the math on 124 or 400 friends. There simply would not be enough time. Yet that is exactly what many evolutionists believe happened. They believe that the world is around 12 million years old, which is not even enough time for a simple protein to line up in the right order, never mind an entire cell. I believe Sir Frederick Hoyle, an astronomer in this century, had it right when he said: "A common-sense interpretation of the facts suggests that a super intellect has monkeyed with physics as well as with chemistry and biology, and that there are no blind forces worth speaking about in nature."

I told you all of this because I wanted you to get just a small glimpse of the extraordinary wonder of God's creation. God is so awesome, and his creation says so. How can we not be amazed? All that God asks of us is to do what he did himself…rest. Imagine that! He wants us to take a break from work and enjoy this wonderful place he created for us. He gave us the Sabbath so that like him, we could sit back to take in the beauty around us and be thankful for our blessings. He gave us a day of rest because we need it spiritually, physically, and emotionally. Our spirits need it so we can realign ourselves with him and be refreshed. Our minds need it so we can de-stress from our busy lives. Our bodies need it so we can be refreshed to face a new week. Taking a day of rest keeps us young and strong in body and mind, and keeps our spirits tuned into his heart. And who wouldn't want that?

DISCUSSION QUESTIONS

"The heavens declare the glory of God; the skies proclaim the work of his hands. Day after day they pour forth speech; night after night they display knowledge." (Psalm 19:1–2)

"But ask the animals, and they will teach you, or the birds of the air, and they will tell you; or speak to the earth, and it will teach you, or let the fish of the sea inform you. Which of all these does not know that the hand of the LORD has done this?" (Job 12:7–9)

1. Read the above scripture. What is it telling you? Do you believe that science and nature declare the work of God, or deny it?
   Answers will vary, but help them to see that all of creation is just too precise not to have a Master Designer.

2. Why did God rest on the seventh day?
   To give us an example to follow, because God knew we would need it, so we can rest and reflect on his goodness to us.

3. Why is resting so important?
   We will live longer and healthier lives if we rest. We need time to reflect on God and his goodness.

4. Since God created everything for us in just six days, what should our gift to him be today?
   Honoring him by resting and reflecting on the Sabbath (the seventh day).

POINTS TO PONDER

What do all of the commonly held scientific theories mean to you? How would you defend your beliefs in intelligent design if you were asked? If you would like to learn more about the evidence that points toward God and his Son, Jesus Christ, I would suggest beginning with author Lee Strobel. He has written many books, and his books *The Case for Creator, The Case for Christ,* and *The Case for Faith* are all available in an easy-to-read Student Edition. This is a great way to build your faith and deepen your understanding along with that of your children.

Another springboard for discussion is the whole concept of Levitical law. If Jesus came to fulfill the law, and honoring God on the Sabbath is a law, do we still need to follow this law? What does that mean to you? What about the other laws?

GIFT

God created this wonderful world for us in six days. On the seventh day he rested. According to Genesis 2:2–3; "By the seventh day God had finished the work he had been doing; so on the seventh day he rested from all his work. And God blessed the seventh day and made it holy, because on it he rested from all the work he had done."

Since even God rested, it is good for us to rest, too. This year, as a gift to him, and to enjoy his presence, commit to keep the Sabbath: to rest, reflect, and keep it holy.

PRAYER

Father in heaven, thank you for this marvelous world you made for us in only six days. Please teach us how to keep the Sabbath in a way that will honor you. Give us wisdom as we plan our busy lives to choose those things that are best and leave room for rest. In Jesus' name, amen.

SUGGESTED ACTIVITIES

OPEN THE SIXTH GIFT BOX AND PLACE THE SIX GEESE-A-LAYING ORNAMENT ON THE TREE.

BRINGING IT HOME TO YOUR HEART

Read the first chapter of Genesis to learn what God created on each day. Remember that he created it for us to enjoy and to bring beauty and fullness to our lives. Take time to write or draw a picture in your journal of your favorite thing that God created. Write God a thank-you note along with it.

At the end of today's lesson and also in Appendix C, we have included some *great* internet links for you and your family. We hope you will take some time to learn a little more about God and his creation through these resources and others mentioned through this book. We truly have an awesome, marvelous God who loves us very much.

BE HIS HANDS AND FEET

Talk with your family about how you can honor God by keeping the Sabbath. Discuss what that would mean. Remember that every family will be different; don't worry if your Sabbath day looks different than someone else's. Ask God what would honor him and work toward that. Decide together what activities you will allow, and how to rest. Also, decide how you will respond when events arise that you choose not to participate in. This should be done in advance so you can honor God and be respectful to others. Record these choices in your journal for easy reference. These choices will not only honor God, but will also bring blessings to your life and family as you learn to rest and play.

These three short videos are well worth watching; even my older children enjoyed them.

http://www.kids4truth.com/eng_creation.htm
http://www.kids4truth.com/watchmaker/watch.html
http://www.kids4truth.com/cv/voice.html

http://www.wayofthemaster.com/evolution.shtml An excellent video on evolution by Kirk Cameron for you and your older children

http://www.jonathanpark.com/ An excellent audio drama series that is creation science based, similar to *Adventures in Odyssey,* great for car trips. They also have great resources and activities for kids on their website.

http://www.apologiaonline.com/conf/ Apologia Educational Ministries Inc. Click on the title of any of the conference handouts to read them.

www.bethlehemstar.net This website is a promo for a fascinating DVD presentation explaining the astronomical phenomenon of the Star of Bethlehem. Although you must purchase the DVD, it is well worth the money and we highly recommend it. The website has some interesting information as well.

THE SEVENTH DAY OF CHRISTMAS

On the seventh day of Christmas, my true love gave to me…
seven swans-a-swimming.

DAY 7, JANUARY 1

SYMBOLISM

The *seven swans-a-swimming* represent the seven gifts of the Holy Spirit: prophecy, ministry, teaching, exhortation, giving, leading, and compassion.

VERSE

We have different gifts, according to the grace given us. If a man's gift is prophesying, let him use it in proportion to his faith. If it is serving, let him serve; if it is teaching, let him teach; if it is encouraging, let him encourage; if it is contributing to the needs of others, let him give gener-ously; if it is leadership, let him govern diligently; if it is showing mercy, let him do it cheerfully. (Romans 12:6–8)

CONCEPT

The seven gifts of the Holy Spirit are given so that we might change from the inside out, to make us ready to do God's work.

TODAY'S STORY

I am sure you all know the story of the ugly duckling; that famous cygnet that grew up to be a beautiful swan. But do you know the rest of the story? If you have ever been to a park or a lake where swans live, you would know that adult swans may be beautiful, but they are not usually nice.

The swan in today's story grew up being rejected because he was not cute like the other ducklings. He spent a lot of time alone, thinking of what it would be like to be beautiful. He so longed to be admired and looked upon with awe, like the other graceful birds on the lake. He realized that could not change his outside appearance, so he focused instead, on what was inside. This swan decided to create gifts of beauty in his heart where no one could see, but he could feel. He searched in his heart, and found those good gifts that he could nurture. He chose to become proficient in things like serving, compassion, and encouragement.

In the spring, after a very long and lonely winter, our little cygnet had grown up. He had spent the winter practicing his new gifts by caring for the other animals that lived on the lake. He had a new confidence about himself; he liked who he had become. He decided to join the others on the lake and care for them as well. After several weeks he could not believe how many friends he had. They all respected and loved him. It was some time later when he looked down and saw his reflection. He discovered that he was indeed a beautiful swan. He realized that God had given him a very valuable gift by keeping his origins a secret for so long. If had he always known that he was a beautiful swan, he may never have attained the strength of character that he achieved.

So it is with us. In our most difficult times, we have a choice. We must choose to let the Spirit develop his gifts in us. Only then can we grow to be more like Jesus.

Oh, and if you ever get a chance to see the swans in the park, and you see one that is more beautiful than the rest, one that is leading the rest with compassion and grace, you will know that this is the famous ugly little duckling.

DISCUSSION QUESTIONS

1. Why should we change from the inside out?
    Because only God can change us on the inside, and that is the only real change.

2. Do you know how you are gifted?
    Answers will vary. Help them to see what gifts they have.

3. Which spiritual gifts do you think you use the most?
    Answers will vary.

POINTS TO PONDER

Another point for discussion is how we all lose our outer beauty in the end. I believe that God did this intentionally. As we become less attractive on the outside it becomes more important to be attractive on the inside. Talk about why it is important to always work on our inner beauty. My dad always told me that pretty on the outside catches them; pretty on the inside keeps them.

GIFT

With Jesus as our Savior, we are gifted with spiritual gifts. Using them is our gift back to Him. Discover your gifts and commit yourself to use them for him and others.

PRAYER

Dear Lord Jesus, thank you for spiritual gifts. Help me to discover mine and use them to the best of my ability. Bless me with more as I use the ones I have. May I honor you with whatever you want me to do. In Jesus' name, amen.

SUGGESTED ACTIVITIES

OPEN THE SEVENTH GIFT BOX AND PLACE THE SEVEN SWANS-A-SWIMMING ORNAMENT ON YOUR TREE.

BRINGING IT HOME TO YOUR HEART

Take a spiritual gifts survey to discover your gifts. There are many surveys on the internet. You can search for one using the key words "spiritual gifts survey" or you can go directly to http://www.kodachrome.org/spiritgift/ and take their test. Commit to using your gifts more. Keep the results in your journal. Review your memory verses and books of the Bible.

BE HIS HANDS AND FEET

Let the Holy Spirit guide you to use your spiritual gifts to bless others this week. Here are just a few suggestions: Write a letter to a soldier to encourage him. Perhaps, as you can afford, you can send him some small gifts to remind him of home. Check Appendix C for ministries that can help you connect with soldiers serving our country overseas. You could also do chores or yard work for someone who is unable to do it themselves. Perhaps you might like to adopt a college student or senior citizen. Try to do something special for someone in your family. Do it secretly. Write in your journal how your recipients reacted and how it blessed both them and you.

THE EIGHTH DAY OF CHRISTMAS

On the eighth day of Christmas, my true love gave to me…
eight maids-a-milking.

DAY 8, JANUARY 2

SYMBOLISM

The *eight maids-a-milking* represent the eight beatitudes as outlined in Matthew 5:8–10.

VERSE

Blessed are the poor in spirit, for theirs is the kingdom of heaven. Blessed are those who mourn, for they will be comforted. Blessed are the meek, for they will inherit the earth. Blessed are those who hunger and thirst for righteousness, for they will be filled. Blessed are the merciful, for they will be shown mercy. Blessed are the pure in heart, for they will see God. Blessed are the peacemakers, for they will be called sons of God. Blessed are those who are persecuted because of righteousness, for theirs is the kingdom of heaven. (Matthew 5:3–10)

CONCEPT

The eight beatitudes are the basic building blocks on which we can grow our faith.

TODAY'S STORY

This is the story of Margaret Gaffney Haughery, the milkmaid of New Orleans. As a little girl, Margaret immigrated with her parents to America from Ireland. A short while later, her parents died, making Margaret an orphan. Sadly, this was not the only tragedy of her life. At the age of twenty-one, she married, and soon gave birth to a baby girl. But within one year, both her husband and baby died. Margaret was truly alone. Despite all the sorrow that permeated her life, she chose to grow in strength and mercy, instead of stagnating in her grief. She learned how to live and to give with a heart of compassion.

During the Great Depression, she obtained work as a laundress at the ritzy St. Charles Hotel in New Orleans. Through the laundry room window, Margaret could see the poor of the city and the people who chose to help them. It was during that time that she decided to make a difference in the lives of others. Before long, she had saved enough money to buy two cows. With only a cart that she pushed by hand, she started selling milk from door to door. Soon she had earned enough money to help a local charity purchase a building for an orphanage.

But Margaret didn't stop there. She also worked many late nights, cleaning and helping to renovate the old building. She continued to grow her milk business until she owned over thirty cows and delivered milk all over the city. One of the stops on her route was a bakery. When the bakery went bankrupt, still owing Margaret quite a bit of money for her milk deliveries, she was given the facility in payment.

Now Margaret found herself in the bread business too. Soon, she was delivering bread to many of her milk customers, as well as to orphanages and charities. Often, she supplied the goods for free or at greatly reduced prices.

By the end of her life, Margaret had helped in the founding of eleven orphanages and several homes for the elderly. She never forgot the lessons she learned early in life: choosing to give instead of wallowing in self-pity. Instead of getting bitter, she chose to get better. What she learned is a good lesson for us today.

DISCUSSION QUESTIONS

1. Why were you put here on this earth?
    To fulfill God's purpose

2. How do we find the purpose for our lives?
    By walking closely to God, reading his Word, praying

3. How can you be a blessing to someone?
    Answers will vary

POINTS TO PONDER

The eight beatitudes are the ways in which we should govern our thoughts. This principle is the basis on which to grow and build our faith. We want to move past mother's milk. "Like newborn babies, crave pure spiritual milk, so that by it you may grow up in your salvation." (1 Peter 2:1–3)

Discuss each of the beatitudes and what they mean.

GIFT

God gave us Jesus, who exemplified the beatitudes. Choose to be like Jesus through the different phases of your life. Think about what it means to live out these attitudes. Choose to act instead of reacting in difficult situations.

PRAYER

Dear Lord Jesus, thank you for giving us the beatitudes. Help me to have your attitude, even in the hard times. Help me to know what to do and to respond correctly in difficult circumstances. In Jesus' name, amen.

SUGGESTED ACTIVITIES

OPEN THE EIGHTH GIFT BOX AND PLACE THE EIGHT MAIDS-A-MILKING ORNAMENT ON YOUR TREE.

BRINGING IT HOME TO YOUR HEART

Work on memorizing the beatitudes. Write in your journal a situation in which you can choose to live one or more of the beatitudes. Review your memory verses and add another as you are ready. At dinner tonight, have each person share three or more things they have been grateful for that day. Try making this a new daily tradition. In this way we change our focus from what we don't have to what we are blessed with.

BE HIS HANDS AND FEET

Write a note of encouragement to someone who has been imprisoned for his faith. Go to www.voiceofthemartyrs.com to write your letter. Pray for him or her. If you have a soup kitchen or facility that feeds the homeless, volunteer to help.

~THE NINTH DAY OF CHRISTMAS~

On the ninth day of Christmas, my true love gave to me...
nine ladies dancing.

DAY 9, JANUARY 3

SYMBOLISM

The *nine ladies dancing* represent the nine fruits of the Holy Spirit: love, joy, peace, patience, kindness, goodness, faithfulness, gentleness, and self-control.

VERSE

But the fruit of the Spirit is love, joy, peace, patience, kindness, goodness, faithfulness, gentleness, and self-control. Against such things there is no law. (Galatians 5:22–23)

CONCEPT

To learn to live by the Spirit and make these character traits a way of life.

TODAY'S STORY

Have you ever been to the ballet? It is an amazing sight of choreographed dancers moving in harmony to the music and each other. In a really good company, the participants move together so beautifully, it almost looks as if they were marionettes, and someone was pulling their strings. Of course, the dancers don't achieve such skill overnight. Becoming a successful ballet dancer takes years of practice to learn the discipline of the dance. There are specific movements that must be mastered and practiced every day so the dancer can stay flexible and graceful.

At this time of year, you will often see companies perform a ballet called *The*

Nutcracker. It is a beautiful ballet about a little girl named Clara who receives a gift of a nutcracker doll from her uncle. When she falls asleep that night, she dreams a fantastic dream in which her nutcracker comes to life as a prince and takes her to his magical kingdom. In her dream, many dancers perform for her. There is one dance after another, each more delightful than the one before. But a sinister rat interrupts their performances, challenging the prince to a duel. Clara is frightened for her prince, but he is victorious, slaying the rat king. The story ends as Clara is awakened and realizes that it was just a dream, but a wonderful dream with a message: don't try to grow up too fast. Enjoy each day as it comes.

For us, there is an even deeper meaning. Let God develop the fruit of his spirit in us every day. These fruits are: love, joy, peace, patience, kindness, goodness, faithfulness, gentleness, and self-control. If you practice these qualities while you are young, allowing God's spirit to nurture them in your heart as you grow physically, you will be able to stand strong in any circumstance. Your life will be gracefully choreographed to the music of his Spirit, beautifully matching the movement of his dance.

DISCUSSION QUESTIONS

1.   What does fruit need to grow?
     Water, sunshine, air

2.   How do we let God grow His fruit in us?
     By praying and expecting him to answer, and instead of just reacting to situations, letting him show us how we should respond.

3.   How do we know his fruit is growing in us?
     We can tell by how well we let the Spirit direct us.

     The Bible says "they will know we are Christians by our love." So we can tell if his fruit is growing in us by our love for one another.

POINTS TO PONDER

King David was known as a man after God's own heart. He also danced for the joy of the Lord in the public streets, for all to see. Can you imagine that kind of abandon, to love God that deeply to make you want to dance?

GIFT

God gave us his Spirit so he could grow fruit in us. This is how we can choose to let him live in and through us. Choose one of the fruits of the Holy Spirit that you are not strong in and ask God to help you to let it blossom.

PRAYER

Dear Lord Jesus, thank you for your fruit, and thank you that your fruit grows in me. Please help me grow more of your good fruit. (love, joy, peace, patience, kindness, goodness, faithfulness, gentleness, and self-control) Help me to dance to your music in my heart. In Jesus' name, amen.

SUGGESTED ACTIVITIES

OPEN THE NINTH GIFT BOX AND PLACE THE NINE LADIES DANCING ORNAMENT ON YOUR TREE.

BRINGING IT HOME TO YOUR HEART

Work on your memory verses. If possible, visit a nursery to see how fruit grows. Ask the gardener about pruning and other measures he takes to produce abundant, healthy fruit. Try to draw a parallel in your own life. What do you need to do to produce good spiritual fruit? If you live near a vineyard, take a tour and see how grapevines are tended. Also, you can attend a live showing of *The Nutcracker* or rent the performance and watch it together as a family. Write in your journal which fruit or fruits you would like to see grow in your life. This is also the reason we put decorative fruit on our Christmas tree.

BE HIS HANDS AND FEET

Deliver a fruit basket or a bottle of sparkling grape juice to someone who needs to sense God's Spirit today. Write a note to someone in your church who helps with the music or dance ministry, thanking them for their hard work. These are just a few ways you can exhibit the fruit of the Spirit.

~ THE TENTH DAY OF CHRISTMAS ~

On the tenth day of Christmas, my true love gave to me…
ten lords-a-leaping.

DAY 10, JANUARY 4

SYMBOLISM

The *ten lords-a-leaping* represent the Ten Commandments.

VERSE

I am the Lord your God, who brought you out of Egypt, out of the land of slavery. You shall have no other gods before me. You shall not make for yourself an idol in the form of anything in heaven above or on the earth beneath or in the waters below. You shall not bow down to them or worship them; for I, the Lord your God, am a jealous God, punishing the children for the sin of the fathers to the third and fourth generation of those who hate me, but showing love to a thousand generations of those who love me and keep my commandments. You shall not misuse the name of the Lord your God, for the Lord will not hold anyone guiltless who misuses his name. Remember the Sabbath day by keeping it holy. Six days you shall labor and do all your work, but the seventh day is a Sabbath to the Lord your God. On it you shall not do any work, neither you, nor your son or daughter, nor your manservant or maidservant, nor your animals, nor the alien within your gates. For in six days the Lord made the heavens and the earth, the sea, and all that is in them, but he rested on the seventh day. Therefore the Lord blessed the Sabbath day and made it holy. Honor your father and your mother, so that you may live long in the land the Lord your God is giving you. You shall not murder. You shall not commit adultery. You shall not steal. You shall not give false testimony against your neighbor. You shall not covet your neighbor's house. You shall not covet your neighbor's wife, or his

manservant or maidservant, his ox or donkey, or anything that belongs to your neighbor.
(Exodus 20:2–17)

CONCEPT

The Ten Commandments were given to help us live at peace with one another and to show
us that we cannot measure up to God and his perfection. They also pointed toward the need
for the sacrificial lamb that was to come.

TODAY'S STORY

Have you ever leapt for joy? The dictionary defines the word leap as *jumping forcefully* or *going up substantially*. So maybe the ten lords-a-leaping were jumping for joy. If they were anything like the Israelites of the Bible, that is exactly what they were doing.

You see, the children of Israel had spent the last 350 years or so in captivity. That means they had been slaves to the Egyptians. They were forced to build their buildings, make their roads, and dig their water systems, all without the help of heavy equipment or quality tools. Everything was accomplished by the manpower of God's chosen people. But, by an amazing set of miracles, God delivered his people out of the hands of the Egyptians. And an awesome deliverance it was. The Israelites jumped for joy as Pharaoh was defeated by God's almighty hand.

Then God sealed his covenant with his people, as he had promised Abraham some six hundred years earlier, by writing down a set of rules: the Ten Commandments. These laws had very specific purposes: to help the people know how to relate to God and to their fellow man. During the time of their captivity, the only example the Israelites had were the Egyptians, who did not acknowledge their God and treated their fellow men as slaves. So God created a set of rules to show the Israelites how they should relate to him and to each other. These commands still apply to us today, and we should learn to live by them.

The first five Commandments speak of how we should relate to God. He is to be number one. Love him and keep his name holy. Do not bow down to anyone or anything else, and set aside a day each week that is just for honoring him.

The final five Commandments show us how to relate to other people. Honor your parents. Be true to your mate. Don't kill, steal, lie, or wish you could have something that belongs to someone else.

These rules were for the Israelites' safety and their happiness. But they were never meant to be the means of their salvation. That would come a thousand years later, with God's son, the Messiah named Jesus. He did not come to do away with the Commandments; rather he kept them, fulfilling them and boiling them all down to two: love God and love man.

However, the Ten Commandments had another, deeper purpose: to show us that we could never be perfect enough. That's why we need Jesus. He was perfectly human, fulfilling God's requirements, and perfectly God, able to deliver us by his sacrificial death on the cross. All we have to do is accept his gift. This is reason enough for all of us to leap for joy!

DISCUSSION QUESTIONS

1. Why are we able to leap for joy?
    Because God sent Jesus for us

2. Which commandment is hardest for you to follow?
    Answers will vary

3. Jesus summarizes the Ten Commandments into just two commands. What are they?
    Love God, love man

ANOTHER POINT FOR DISCUSSION;

We couldn't close this chapter without taking this opportunity to ask: *Are you right with God? What about your children?* Take time to read the following page to make sure you are right according to his standards. It will only take a few minutes, and it could change your life and make an eternal difference. Most people believe that they are basically good people. How about you? Well, it really doesn't matter what we think. God is the ultimate judge, and as you read in the last story, he has a very high standard.

1. Have you ever told a lie? Even if it was a little white one or a half-truth? Then what does that say you are? God says you are a liar.

2. Have you ever stolen anything? Maybe it was something small, like a pencil or a piece of gum or even unintentionally borrowing something from someone and forgetting to return it. What does that make you? According to God's law, you are a thief.

3. Have you ever wished you had something that you don't have? Or have you ever worked on the Sabbath? Or dishonored your parents? Then you are a coveter, a law breaker and a sinner. The Bible clearly states that there is no one righteous, No, not *one*. So are you good enough according to God's Law?

"Now we know that whatever the law says, it says to those who are under the law, so that every mouth may be silenced and the whole world held accountable to God. Therefore no one will be declared righteous in his sight by observing the law; rather, through the law we became conscious of sin." (Romans 3:19, 20)

According to what you now know, if you stand before God, are you guilty or innocent? There is no middle ground. To God, this issue is totally black or white. You are either completely innocent or completely guilty.

Let's put it this way: Say you were at school and you were making fun of one of your classmates. You thought the other child could not hear you, and you said some awfully unkind things. As you were saying one of the rude things, the child you were speaking of suddenly came around the corner and you realized he could hear you the whole time.

Just then, your teacher arrived on the scene and marched the two of you to the principal's office.

Your teacher told the principal the whole story. He looked at you and said, "Is this true? Are you guilty?"

You know that if you tell the truth, you will have to do two months of community service. As a just and kind principal, he must obey the rules of the school and sentence you. In fact, you wouldn't want it any other way because a good principal wouldn't let unjust behavior go unpunished. You know you are guilty and must pay the price. Just as your sentencing takes place, your best friend who is the student council president walks in the room.

"Wait!" he says. "I have already done his community service for him. His debt is paid. He is able to go free if he will promise not to do this again."

Would you accept his payment for your wrongdoing? This is what Jesus did for us.

Heaven is a perfect place. Should God let liars and thieves into his perfect place? We are all guilty. The law was given so we could see ourselves as he sees us, and show us our need for a savior. It points out our sins and humbles us as we realize we can never measure up. Unless we are humble, we have no need for the saving grace of God that he provided through Jesus Christ. Jesus took upon himself the punishment for your sins and for mine. He was the perfect sacrifice provided by God because he loves us so much. Without him, there would be no way for us to reconcile with God. God is like the principal in our story. And Jesus did our community service.

So what should you do?

First, realize that you are guilty. Humbly go before him and admit your guilt. Why not make Psalm 51 your prayer. From this day forward trust him to guide your life and accept Jesus as the sacrifice for your sin. Then thank him for Jesus, who took our place, taking our punishment upon himself. Romans 5:8 says, "But God demonstrates his own love for us in this: while we were still sinners, Christ died for us."

PSALM 51:

1. Have mercy on me, O God,
according to your unfailing love;
according to your great compassion
blot out my transgressions.

2. Wash away all my iniquity
and cleanse me from my sin.

3. For I know my transgressions,
and my sin is always before me.

4. Against you, you only, have I sinned
and done what is evil in your sight,
so that you are proved right when you speak
and justified when you judge.

5. Surely I was sinful at birth,

sinful from the time my mother conceived me.

6. Surely you desire truth in the inner parts;
you teach me wisdom in the inmost place.

7. Cleanse me with hyssop, and I will be clean;
wash me, and I will be whiter than snow.

8. Let me hear joy and gladness;
let the bones you have crushed rejoice.

9. Hide your face from my sins
and blot out all my iniquity.

10. Create in me a pure heart, O God,
and renew a steadfast spirit within me.

11. Do not cast me from your presence
or take your Holy Spirit from me.

12. Restore to me the joy of your salvation
and grant me a willing spirit, to sustain me.

13. Then I will teach transgressors your ways,
and sinners will turn back to you.

14. Save me from bloodguilt, O God,
the God who saves me,
and my tongue will sing of your righteousness.

15. O Lord, open my lips,
and my mouth will declare your praise.

16. You do not delight in sacrifice, or I would bring it;
you do not take pleasure in burnt offerings.

17. The sacrifices of God are a broken spirit;
a broken and contrite heart,
O God, you will not despise.

18. In your good pleasure make Zion prosper;
build up the walls of Jerusalem.

19. Then there will be righteous sacrifices,
whole burnt offerings to delight you;
then bulls will be offered on your altar.

GIFT

Our gift to him today is to praise God for his wisdom in providing the Ten Commandments for our protection and freedom by cheerfully obeying them. Commit them to your heart.

PRAYER

Thank you, Father, that you planned on sending Jesus long before we knew we needed you. Thank you, Jesus, for being willing to come to earth, and especially for being willing to die for me, even before I realized I needed you. In Jesus' name, amen

SUGGESTED ACTIVITIES

OPEN THE TENTH GIFT BOX AND PLACE THE TEN LORDS-A-LEAPING ORNAMENT ON YOUR TREE.

BRINGING IT HOME TO YOUR HEART

Write the Ten Commandments on a scroll (Appendix B). Memorize them and write them in your journal. Review your memory verses from previous days. Make a plaque for your doorpost with the Ten Commandments on it and hang it on your door. Find out which government buildings post the Ten Commandments in public. Visit one and pray for the people who work there to know the richness of God's laws and his love for them.

BE HIS HANDS AND FEET

Make a list of our government officials that you can pray for. Create a prayer journal to record your concerns for them and the results of those prayers. Write letters to your leaders and let them know you are praying for them.

THE ELEVENTH DAY OF CHRISTMAS

On the eleventh day of Christmas, my true love gave to me…
eleven pipers piping.

DAY 11, JANUARY 5

SYMBOLISM

The *eleven pipers piping* represent the 11 faithful disciples who are: 1) Simon Peter 2)Andrew 3)James 4)John 5)Philip 6)Bartholomew 7)Matthew 8)Thomas 9)James son of Alpheus 10)Simon the Zealot and 11) Thaddaeus

VERSE

These are the twelve he appointed: Simon (to whom he gave the name Peter), James son of Zebedee and his brother John (to them he gave the name Boanerges, which means Sons of Thunder), Andrew, Philip, Bartholomew, Matthew, Thomas, James bar Alpheus, Thaddaeus, Simon the Zealot, and Judas Iscariot, who betrayed him. (Mark 3:16–19)

CONCEPT

Of Jesus' twelve disciples, eleven were loyal and one betrayed him. We must choose to remain faithful to him, like the faithful eleven.

TODAY'S STORY

Today's story is about a musician and his life changing music. It happened long ago and far away, and you will probably be familiar with some of the story. If you listen carefully, you may even be able to imagine yourself in it.

Once there was a musician. He wasn't an ordinary music maker who played for paying audiences only; no, this musician was famous throughout the land as one who would play his instrument for anyone who would listen. He especially loved playing for children, for their hearts were particularly open to his melody. His instrument was special too. It was a silver flute with intricately-carved designs on it. It looked as if it were very old and made by a skilled craftsman of another time.

One day, the musician arose early and began walking and playing his flute. The melody was so pure that it almost sounded as if someone was singing. People in the nearby village came out of their houses to see where the beautiful sound was coming from. As the musician approached the village, all the children came running, for he had created this song especially for them. At first, the parents didn't realize who was making the music, but as he entered the village, they looked into his eyes and heard his melody. They knew that this was the famous musician they had heard of, and that he meant them no harm.

The children danced and sang with all their hearts as the musician led them through town. One boy loved the music so much that he wiggled his way all the way to the front of the group, closest to the music-maker. He felt a little funny dancing in front of everyone, but he felt drawn to the musician and wanted to please him. He followed closely, copying every move that the musician made. His heart beat a little faster when the musician looked at him and smiled. He followed for a long time, trying to mimic every move, every smile, and every nuance of the musician.

Suddenly, the music stopped. The musician turned to the little boy and handed him the flute. The boy could not believe it! He put the flute to his lips and blew. Beautiful music came pouring from the instrument. He was stunned. The children all cheered and danced, following and mimicking the little boy. Then they started begging to have a turn, too. The little boy ignored them and continued to play. The musician smiled at the boy, bent down, and whispered something in his ear. The boy frowned, but reluctantly handed the coveted flute to someone else.

He listened as the other child began to play. He loved the music and song, and he wanted to dance like the others, but he suddenly didn't want to be seen acting like that. After all, he was too old for those silly games. *They look ridiculous,* he thought as he followed at a safe distance. But the music still beckoned him.

Then all of a sudden, he heard his name in the music. The musician was looking directly at him, playing the flute, yet calling him. The boy was mesmerized. The other children didn't seem to notice, for they were still dancing and singing along. He felt his face go hot. *I'm goin' fishin',* he thought. And he turned and walked away. The musician continued to call, but the boy hardened his heart, and in his stubborn pride, ran to his favorite fishing hole.

Meanwhile, the musician led the children into a clearing where a delicious feast was waiting. The children had never seen so much scrumptious food. There was roasted meat and vegetables, and fruit of all kinds. There were delicious cakes and steaming hot mugs of cocoa. Presently, the musician gave the cue, and the feasting began. The children laughed and ate and drank until their hearts and tummies were content.

The musician laughed and played with the children all day. He played them a lullaby in the afternoon and they all rested in the soft grass. As they settled down, the musician's thoughts returned to the little boy who would not come, and he felt a twinge of sadness in his heart.

At that very same moment, as the boy was walking home from fishing, he thought of the musician, and he too felt a sad longing in his heart. For he knew that his moment for choosing and being chosen had passed, and he had made the wrong choice.

DISCUSSION QUESTIONS

1. Who does Jesus long for a relationship with?
    All of us, me

2. What does it mean to you, that Jesus wants a relationship with you?
    Answers will vary, but the bottom line is that he loved us while we were still sinners

3. What can you do about it?
    Give him my life and seek him with all my heart

POINTS TO PONDER

Another point for discussion is that we want to be one of the eleven faithful not the one betrayer. The disciples all had a song to sing, a story to tell that led people to Christ. What will your song be to have people follow you to Jesus?

GIFT

God is always faithful to us. Like the eleven faithful disciples, we must choose to remain faithful to him. You can do this by committing to spend time with him on a regular basis. Use a devotional guide or a Bible reading plan and read every day, either by yourself or together with your family. Talk to him, too.

PRAYER

Dear Lord Jesus, thank you for the gift of music. And thank you that when I listen carefully, I can hear your song in my heart. Help me to listen and respond to your music. In Jesus' name, amen.

OPEN THE ELEVENTH GIFT BOX AND HANG THE ELEVEN PIPERS PIPING ORNAMENT ON YOUR TREE.

BRINGING IT HOME TO YOUR HEART

Memorize the names of the twelve disciples. They are: 1) Simon Peter 2) Andrew 3) James 4) John 5) Philip 6) Bartholomew 7) Matthew 8) Thomas 9) James bar (son of) Alpheus 10) Simon the Zealot 11) Thaddaeus and 12) Judas Iscariot who betrayed Jesus. Write them in your journal. Learn something about the character of one or more of the disciples. Pantomime something about them and have a friend guess who you are. Review your other memory work, too.

BE HIS HANDS AND FEET

Jesus' disciples followed him wherever he went. They assisted him in his tasks and met the needs of those around them as Jesus healed the sick and loved the unlovely. Today, think of some way you can be like his disciples and meet a need of someone you know. Ask your mom if you could help her around the house, or do something without being asked. Play a game or read a book with a younger brother or sister. Begin to make a habit of doing an unexpected act of service every day. Then as a family you can each share your act of service for the day at dinner time. You could also take some of your unused toys or clothing to an agency where they can be given to those who will use them. Make or purchase items to give to someone in need. You don't have to do all these things at once, but begin to make a deliberate practice of being his disciple.

~ THE TWELFTH DAY OF CHRISTMAS ~

On the twelfth day of Christmas, my true love gave to me…
twelve drummers drumming.

DAY 12, JANUARY 6, EPIPHANY

SYMBOLISM

The *twelve drummers drumming* represent the twelve tenants of our faith as outlined in the Apostle's Creed.

VERSE

The Twelve Points of the Apostles' Creed

1. I believe in God, the Father Almighty, creator of heaven and earth.
2. I believe in Jesus Christ, his only Son, our Lord.
3. He was conceived by the power of the Holy Spirit and born of the Virgin Mary.
4. He suffered under Pontius Pilate, was crucified, died, and was buried. He descended into the grave.
5. On the third day he rose again. He ascended into heaven and is seated at the right hand of God the Father.
6. He will come again to judge the living and the dead.
7. I believe in the Holy Spirit,
8. Christ's Bride, the Holy Church (which means the entire body of believers in Christ)
9. The communion of the saints,
10. The forgiveness of sins,
11. The resurrection of the body
12. And life everlasting.

CONCEPT

As Christians, we all share the same faith in Jesus Christ, so we are all brothers and sisters.

TODAY'S STORY

For our final day together, imagine with me if you will, music without rhythm. No drums, no timing, no force to keep it from wandering wherever and whenever it wants. Instead of music, it would be a cacophony of notes. Can you imagine a drummer trying to play without keeping a beat? It would only be an obnoxious noise of banging and crashing and clanging.

Once when we were at an amusement park, we saw a stomp band. At first, it just seemed like a noisy guy banging on an overturned bucket. But soon, several others joined in; one on a trash can, another on a plastic pail and another on a trash can lid, all of it syncopated by the whoops and hollers of the players. It was amazing. They played on ordinary objects, yet had an extraordinary sound. It was banging, crashing and clanging, but it was all done in rhythm, and so it became music.

In a marching band, the drum line keeps everyone together. They keep the music in rhythm and the steps in place. The drum major sets the tempo (the speed of the music), and the drummers follow the beat he leads. They must keep their eyes on the drum major at all times, so they will know how fast or slow the music should go. If the drummers falter, the whole band gets lost and the music turns to noise.

That's how our lives are. We must keep our eyes on Jesus all the time, following his leadership, and taking his direction for our lives. We must live our lives in rhythm with his heartbeat, so that we will be in harmony with the other believers around us. If we do not, our testimony will just sound like noise to others.

How do we hear God's heartbeat rhythm? By reading his Word and putting what it says into practice in our lives. We also need to pray and listen. God does speak to us by his Holy Spirit, but we are often too busy to hear him. He also speaks to us through our circumstances and through other godly people. As a kid, your parents, even if they are not Christians, can be a great source to help you hear what God has to say. It is also helpful to memorize scripture. Then, when you are in a situation where you don't know what to do, you can whisper a prayer and rely on God's Word, even if you don't have a Bible with you.

It all comes from the heart. It comes down from the Father's heart, to the Son's, and then on to his adopted ones. This rhythm creates the most beautiful life, one that is well lived and remembered long after it is over.

DISCUSSION QUESTIONS

1. What is the most important thing that all people should believe?
    Jesus Christ is our Savior

2. How is this going to make a difference in your life this year?
    Answers will vary

3. What is the thing you remember most about the last twelve days?
   Answers vary

POINT TO PONDER

Now that the twelve days are complete, what is the most important principle that you would like to carry with you into this new year as a family, and individually? Have everyone give their thoughts and than decide together. May you have a blessed year.

GIFT

We have arrived at our final gift for our Savior. This is not really the final gift, but just the beginning; a lifelong gift of praise and worship. The psalmist said it this way:

> Let the heavens rejoice, let the earth be glad;
> let the sea resound, and all that is in it;
> let the fields be jubilant, and everything in them.
> Then all the trees of the forest will sing for joy.
> (Psalm 96:11,12)

We need to believe, not just that he exists, but trust in all that he says, all that he is, and all that he does. We need to realize our need for him as our Savior, and accept his gift of grace to us. God wants to have a relationship with us. He gave his Son for us and created an amazing world for us to live in. He gave us his Word and his Holy Spirit to guide us on our way. Our gift to him is to believe, worship, and follow him now and throughout the rest of our lives.

PRAYER

Dear Lord Jesus, thank you for the past year that we have brought to a close and this new year we are just beginning. Thank you for your Son who gave everything for us. Thank you for your Word and the Holy Spirit you sent to guide us. Help us listen and obey. Thank you for the world and everything you created for us to enjoy. Help us to remember you and your rhythm in our lives in all situations. In Jesus' name, amen.

OPEN THE LAST GIFT BOX AND PLACE THE TWELVE DRUMMERS DRUMMING ORNAMENT ON YOUR TREE.

BRINGING IT HOME TO YOUR HEART

Read the *Apostles' Creed* and discuss each point. In your journal, write each point in your own words. Review all your memory work and congratulate yourself for a job well done. Remember too, that the angels are rejoicing for you.

BE HIS HANDS AND FEET

Today is Epiphany, or Three Kings Day.

Make a Three Kings Cake and invite neighbors or friends over for a Three Kings Party. Be creative; share your journal and what you have learned with your friends. Celebrate all God has done for you in the past twelve days, and look forward to what he is going to accomplish in and through you in this new year. Be sure to send us an email that tells us how you liked this guide and what suggestions you may have. We look forward to hearing what God is doing in you.

APPENDICES

Appendix A	Appendix B	Appendix C
List of Memory Verses	Scrolls for the 12 gifts	Websites for:
Bounce Back Game for scripture memory	Coloring pages	Armed Forces Ministries
	Twelve Days Music	Voice of the Martyrs
Prophecy Matching Game	Birdfeeder instructions	Compassion International
Obedience Game	The Golden Rule	World Vision
Three Kings Party Guide: instructions and games	The Five Golden Rules of Obedience	Samaritan's Purse
	Golden Bundt Cake recipes	Local Government Addresses website
	Table of Gifts	Link for Day Two
	Ten Commandment Scroll and Plaque instructions	Link for Day six
	The Ten Commandments (complete and simplified versions)	
	Three Kings Cake recipes	

<h1 style="text-align:center">APPENDIX A</h1>

MEMORY VERSES

DAY 1

John 3:16

For God so loved the world that he gave his one and only Son, that whoever believes in him shall not perish but have eternal life.

John 4:10

Jesus answered her, "If you knew the gift of God and who it is that asks you for a drink, you would have asked him and he would have given you living water."

DAY 2

Luke 2:22–24

When the time of their purification according to the Law of Moses had been completed, Joseph and Mary took him to Jerusalem to present him to the Lord, (as it is written in the Law of the Lord, "Every firstborn male is to be consecrated to the Lord") and to offer a sacrifice in keeping with what is said in the Law of the Lord: "a pair of doves or two young pigeons."

Isaiah 53:11–12

After the suffering of his soul, he will see the light of life and be satisfied; by his knowledge my righteous servant will justify many, and he will bear their iniquities.

Therefore I will give him a portion among the great, and he will divide the spoils with the strong, because he poured out his life unto death, and was numbered with the transgressors. For he bore the sin of many, and made intercession for the transgressors.

DAY 3

Matthew 2:10–11

When they saw the star, they were overjoyed. On coming to the house, they saw the child with his mother Mary, and they bowed down and worshiped him. Then they opened their treasures and presented him with gifts of gold and of incense and of myrrh.

1 Corinthians 13:13

And now these three remain: faith, hope and love. But the greatest of these is love.

DAY 4

John 20:31

But these are written that you may believe that Jesus is the Christ, the Son of God, and that by believing you may have life in his name.

1 Thessalonians 1:5

Because our gospel came to you not simply with words, but also with power, with the Holy Spirit and with deep conviction. You know how we lived among you for your sake.

DAY 5

Psalm 19:9–10

The fear of the LORD is pure, enduring forever. The ordinances of the LORD are sure and altogether righteous.

They are more precious than gold, than much pure gold; they are sweeter than honey, than honey from the comb.

Psalm 119:127–128

Because I love your commands more than gold, more than pure gold, and because I consider all your precepts right, I hate every wrong path.

DAY 6

Genesis 1:1

In the beginning God created the heavens and the earth.

Romans 1:20

For since the creation of the world God's invisible qualities—his eternal power and divine nature—have been clearly seen, being understood from what has been made, so that men are without excuse.

DAY 7

Romans 12:6–8

We have different gifts, according to the grace given us. If a man's gift is prophesying, let him use it in proportion to his faith. If it is serving, let him serve; if it is teaching, let him teach; if it is encouraging, let him encourage; if it is contributing to the needs of others, let him give generously; if it is leadership, let him govern diligently; if it is showing mercy, let him do it cheerfully.

1 Corinthians 12: 8–12

To one there is given through the Spirit the message of wisdom, to another the message of knowledge by means of the same Spirit, to another faith by the same Spirit, to another gifts of healing by that one Spirit, to another miraculous powers, to another prophecy, to another distinguishing between spirits, to another speaking in different kinds of tongues, and to still another the interpretation of tongues. All these are the work of one and the same Spirit, and he gives them to each one, just as he determines.

The body is a unit, though it is made up of many parts; and though all its parts are many, they form one body. So it is with Christ.

DAY 8

Matthew 5: 3–10

Blessed are the poor in spirit, for theirs is the kingdom of heaven.
Blessed are those who mourn, for they will be comforted.
Blessed are the meek, for they will inherit the earth.
Blessed are those who hunger and thirst for righteousness, for they will be filled.
Blessed are the merciful, for they will be shown mercy.
Blessed are the pure in heart, for they will see God.
Blessed are the peacemakers, for they will be called sons of God.
Blessed are those who are persecuted because of righteousness, for theirs is the kingdom of heaven.

2 Thessalonians 3:13

But as for you, brethren, do not grow weary of doing good.

DAY 9

Galatians 5:22, 23

But the fruit of the Spirit is love, joy, peace, patience, kindness, goodness, faithfulness, gentleness and self-control. Against such things there is no law.

Galatians 5:25–26

Since we live by the Spirit, let us keep in step with the Spirit. Let us not become conceited, provoking and envying each other.

DAY 10

Deuteronomy 7:9

Know therefore that the LORD your God is God; he is the faithful God, keeping his covenant of love to a thousand generations of those who love him and keep his commands.

Exodus 20:2–17

I am the LORD your God, who brought you out of Egypt, out of the land of slavery.

You shall have no other gods before me.

You shall not make for yourself an idol in the form of anything in heaven above or on the earth beneath or in the waters below. You shall not bow down to them or worship them; for I, the LORD your God, am a jealous God, punishing the children for the sin of the fathers to the third and fourth generation of those who hate me, but showing love to a thousand generations of those who love me and keep my commandments.

You shall not misuse the name of the LORD your God, for the LORD will not hold anyone guiltless who misuses his name.

Remember the Sabbath day by keeping it holy. Six days you shall labor and do all your work, but the seventh day is a Sabbath to the LORD your God. On it you shall not do any work, neither you, nor your son or daughter, nor your manservant or maidservant, nor your animals, nor the alien within your gates. For in six days the LORD made the heavens and the earth, the sea, and all that is in them, but he rested on the seventh day. Therefore the LORD blessed the Sabbath day and made it holy.

Honor your father and your mother, so that you may live long in the land the LORD your God is giving you.

You shall not murder.

You shall not commit adultery.

You shall not steal.

You shall not give false testimony against your neighbor.

You shall not covet your neighbor's house. You shall not covet your neighbor's wife, or his manservant or maidservant, his ox or donkey, or anything that belongs to your neighbor.

DAY 11

Mark 3:16–19

These are the twelve he appointed: Simon (to whom he gave the name Peter), James son of Zebedee and his brother John (to them he gave the name Boanerges, which means Sons of Thunder), Andrew, Philip, Bartholomew, Matthew, Thomas, James son of Alphaeus, Thaddaeus, Simon the Zealot and Judas Iscariot, who betrayed him.

Mark 8:34

Then he called the crowd to him along with his disciples and said: "If anyone would come after me, he must deny himself and take up his cross and follow me.

DAY 12

Apostles Creed

1. I believe in God, the Father Almighty, creator of heaven and earth.
2. I believe in Jesus Christ, his only Son, our Lord.
3. He was conceived by the power of the Holy Spirit and born of the Virgin Mary.
4. He suffered under Pontius Pilate, was crucified, died, and was buried. He descended into the grave.
5. On the third day he rose again. He ascended into heaven and is seated at the right hand of
6. God the Father.
7. He will come again to judge the living and the dead.
8. I believe in the Holy Spirit,
9. Christ's Bride, the Holy Church (which means the entire body of believers in Christ)
10. The communion of the saints,
11. The forgiveness of sins,
12. The resurrection of the body
13. And life everlasting.

Romans 7:4

So, my brothers, you also died to the law through the body of Christ, that you might belong to another, to him who was raised from the dead, in order that we might bear fruit to God.

1 Corinthians 15:1

Now, brothers, I want to remind you of the gospel I preached to you, which you received and on which you have taken your stand.

BOUNCE BACK GAME INSTRUCTIONS

This is an easy way to memorize anything, especially scripture. It can be played with two or more people. For two people, the first person says the first word in the verse to be memorized. The second person says the second word. Then it "bounces back" to the first person again, who says the third word. Then it "bounces back" to the second person again. Continue this pattern until the verse is finished. For more people, go from the first person, to the second, to the third, and so forth. If someone is unable to say their word, the next person says it, or helps the person remember.

Variation #1 is played like the original, except a person is picked to be the "bouncer." This person says the first word, and then points to another player who says the second word. Then it goes back to the bouncer, who says the third word and points to someone else for the fourth. Continue this pattern until the verse is finished.

Variation #2 is a little different. Stand in a circle, (for two people, facing each other) and the first person says the first word. The second person has to repeat the first word and say the second. The third player says the first and second word, then the third. Play continues this way until the verse is done.

PROPHECY MATCHING GAME

Match prophecies from the Old Testament on the left, to the fulfillment in the New Testament on the right. Answers are on the page that follows.

We have provided you with a chart of prophecies of who the Messiah must be with the source of the prophecy in the Old Testament and the fulfillment in the New Testament.

There are many ways to use these. We have included instructions for several games. Feel free to make up your own. If you do, email them to us and we will include them on our website.

Game 1:

This game is played like "Memory." Make a copy of the Matching game on the following pages. Choose the ones you want to use and cut those out. Place them face down on a table, Old Testament on one side and New Testament on the other. Keep them separate. Get out your Bible, then turn over one prophecy on the left and one on the right. Look up the scriptures and see if they match. If they do, take another turn. If not, return them to the table and your turn ends. The winner is the one with the most matches. You could also copy the prophecy and the verse on index cards and play with those.

Game 2

This game is also played like "Memory" with a twist. For this game, you will need to use 3x5 cards. Choose about five (or more, depending on the ages of your children and their knowledge of the scriptures) prophesies and copy the reference on the front side of the card and its verse on the back, making a total of ten cards; five from the Old Testament, and the matching five from the New. Turn all the cards with the reference up, then try to say the verse from memory and what its matching prophecy is. Then try to match it with its partner. If you can say the verse, you win that set. Alternately, you could prepare the cards as instructed, but instead of quoting the scripture, you choose the card and read the scripture, then state the prophecy that it fulfills, find its match and verify by reading the scripture. If you are correct, you keep the match. Winner is the one with the most matches at the end.

Game 3
You can easily create a "matching page" for older students to complete independently. On the right side of the page, list five to ten scripture references from the Old Testament. On the left side, list the matching reference from the New Testament in mixed up order. Have students draw a line from right side to the matching scripture on the left. As they look up the scripture, have them write what the scripture prophesies next to the reference. Alternately, list the Old Testament reference on the left and the New Testament scripture verse on the right. Or you could mix Old and New Testament references on the left and their matching verses on the right. There are many other ways you could do this. Use your imagination and enjoy!

Game 4
Make several copies of the blank BINGO card in Appendix A. (Our BINGO card says JESUS at the top.) Copy the Prophesy Matching Game pages and cut them up, but keep them in order. Use matching Old and New Testament scripture and their prophecy in various spots on the board. Fill in all the spots, then copy. Make up several cards varying the scriptures slightly, and putting them in different spots. Make several copies (some for now and some for later!) Play like BINGO by calling out the scripture reference, the actual verse, or the prophecy. If they have it on the card, they can mark as many as match.

Prophecy: The Messiah Must	Source in The Old Testment	Fulfillment in the New Testment
Be the "seed of the woman" that would "bruise" or "crush" the serpent"s "head"	Genesis 3:15	Galatians 4:4 1 John 3:8
Be the seed of "Abraham"	Genesis 12:3	Matthew 1:1, Acts 3:25 Galatians 3:16
Be the seed of Isaac	Genesis 17:19, 21:12	Matthew 1:2 Luke 3:34 Hebrews 11:17-19
Be the "seed of Jacob" and the "star out of Jacob" who will have Dominion	Genesis 28:14 Numbers 24:17,19	Matthew 1:2 Luke 3:34 Revelation 22:16
Be a descendant of Judah	Genesis 49:10	Matthew 1:2-3 Luke 3:33 Hebrews 7:14
Be a descendant of David and heir to his throne	2 Samuel 7:12-13 Isaiah 9:6(7), 11:1-5 Jeremiah 23:5	Matthew 1:1,6 Acts 13:22-23 Romans 1:3
Have eternal existence	Micah 5:1(2)	John 1:1,14 8:58 Ephesians 1:3-4 Colossians 1:15-19 Revelation 1:18
Be the Son of God	Psalm 2:7 Proverbs 30:4	Mathew 3:17 Luke 1:32
Have God's own name applied to Him	Isaiah 9:5-6(6-7) Jeremiah 23:5-6	Romans 10:9 Philippians 2:9-11
Come 69x7 years (483 years) after the rebuilding of the wall of Jerusalem	Daniel 9:24-26	Matthew 2:1 16, 19 Luke 3:1, 23
Be born of a virgin	Isaiah 7:14	Matthew 1:18-2:1 Luke 1:26-35
Be born in Bethleham in Judah	Micah 5:1(2)	Matthew 2:1 Luke 2:4-7
Be adored by great persons	Paslm 72:10-11	Matthew 2:1-11
Be preceded by one who would announce Him	Isaiah 40:3-5 Malachi 3:1	Matthew 3:1-3 Luke 1:17, 3:2-6
Be anointed with the Spirit of God	Isaiah 11:2, 61:1 Psalm 45: 8(7)	Matthew 3:16 John 3:34 Acts 10:38

Prophecy: The Messiah Must	Source in The Old Testment	Fulfillment in the New Testament
Be a prophet like Moses	Deuteronomy 18:15, 18	Acts 3:20-22
Have a ministry of binding up the brokenhearted, proclaiming liberty to the captives and announcing the acceptable year of the Lord	Isaiah 61:1-2	Luke 4:18-19
Have a ministry of Healing	Isaiah 35:5-6, 42:18	Matthew 11:5 throught the Gospels
Have a ministry in the Galil	Isaiah 8:23-9:1(2)	Matthew 4:12-16
Be tender and compassionate	Isaiah 40:11, 42:3	Matthew 12:15, 20 Hebrews 4:15
Be meek and unostentatious	Isaiah 42:2	Matthew 21:15-15, 19
Be sinless and without guile	Isaiah 53:9	1 Peter 2:22
Bear the repoaches due others	Isaiah 53:11-12 Psalm 69:10(9)	Romans 15:3
Be a priest	Psalm 110:4	Hebrews 5:5-6, 6:20, 7:15-17
Enter publicly into Jerusalem on a donkey	Zechariah 9:9	Matthew 21:1-11 Mark 11:1-11
Enter the Temple with authority	Malachi 3:1	Matthew 21:12-24:1 Luke 2:27-38, 45-50 John 2:13-22
Be Hated without cause	Isaiah 49:7 Psalm 69:5(4)	John 15:24-25
Be undesired and rejected by his own people	Isaiah 53:2-3 63:3,5 Psalm 69:9(8)	Mark 6:3 Luke 9:58 John 1:11 7:3-5
Be rejected by the Jewish leadership	Psalm 118:22	Matthew 21:42 John 7:48
Be plotted against by Jews and Gentiles together	Psalm 2:1-2	Act 4:27
Be betrayed by a friend	Psalm 41:10(9) 55:13-15(12-14)	Matthew 26:21-25, 47-50 John 13:18-21, Act 1:16-18
Be sold for 30 pieces of silver	Zechariah 11:12	Matthew 26:15
Have His price given for a potter's field	Zechariah 11:13	Matthew 27:6-7

Prophecy: The Messiah Must	Source in The Old Testment	Fulfillment in the New Testment
Be forsaken by His student	Zechariah 13:7	Matthew 26:31,56
Be struck on the cheek	Micah 4:14(5:1)	Matthew 27:30
Be spat on	Isaiah 50:6	Matthew 26:67 ; 27:30
Be mocked	Psalm 22;8-9(7-8)	Matthew 26:67-68; 27:31, 39-44
Be beaten	Isaiah 50:6	Matthew 26:67; 27:26, 30
Be executed by crucifixion,	Psalm 22:17(16)	Matthew 27:35 Luke 24:39
by having His hands and feet piecrced	Zecharaiah 12:10	John 19:18, 34-37, 20:20-28 Revelation 1:7
Be thirsty during his execution	Psalm 22:16(15)	John 19:28
Be given vinegar to quench that thirst	Psalm 69:22(21)	Matthew 27:34
Be executed without having a bone broken	Exodus 12:46 Psalm 34:21(20)	John 19:33-36
Be considered a transgressor	Isiash 53:12	Matthew 27:3
Be "cut off, but not for himself," 69x7 years after rebuilding of the wall of Jerusalem	Daniel 9:24-26	Romans 5:16 1Peter 3:3:18
Be the one whose death would atone for sins of mankind	Isaiah 53:5-7, 12	Mark 10:45 John 1:29, 3:16 Acts 8:30-35
Be buried with the rich when dead	Isaiah 53:9	Matthew 27:57-60
Be raised from the dead	Isaiah 53:9-10 Psalm 2:7, 16:10	Matthew 28:1-20 Acts 2:23-36, 13:33-37 1Corinthians 15:4-6
Ascend to the right hand of God	Psalm 16:11, 68:19(18), 110:1	Luke 24:51, Act 1:9-11, 7:55 Hebrews 1:3
Exercise his priestly office in heaven	Zechariah 6:13	Romans 8:34 Hebrews 7:25-8:2
Be the cornerstone of God's Messianic Community	Isaiah 28:16 Psalm 118:22-23	Matthew 21:42 Ephesians 2:20, 1 Peter 2;5-7
Be sought after by Gentiles as well as Jews	Isaiah 11:10, 42:1	Acts 10:45-46 13:46-48
Be accepted by the Gentiles	Isaiah 11:10,42:1-4, 49:1-6	Matthew 12:18-21 Romans 9:30, 10:20, 11:11, 15:10
Be the king	Psalm 2:6	John 18:33,37
Be seen by Isreal as pierced	Zechariah 12:10 Psalm 22:17(16)	Luke 24:39 John 19:34-37 Revelation 1:7

J	E	S	U	S

OBEDIENCE GAME, OTHERWISE KNOWN AS *O-B-E-Y*

This game is similar to "four corners" and is best played with a fairly large group of children. Designate all four corners, each with one letter of the word "obey." Then, stand in the center of the room with all the children and yell, "1, 2, 3, Obey!" The children will all run to a corner. While they are running, close your eyes and count to ten, then shout out either O, B, E, or Y. The children in the corner that you called are out. When four children or less are left, each child must choose a separate corner. Play is continued until only one child is left, and he is declared "the most obedient."

Variation: This game can also be played outside, with trees or other landmarks as the corners.

THREE KINGS PARTY GUIDE

Just like the Magi celebrated when they found the Baby Jesus, the Three Kings party should be a celebration of the Twelve Days of Christmas journey. Brainstorm with your children to come up with things to do. Here are a few ideas:

- Light your advent candle and explain to the children why the Magi brought the gifts they did to baby Jesus. There is no clear-cut Biblical explanation, but it is speculated that the gold was to finance their flight from Egypt, the frankincense was a fragrant offering like that used by the priests in the temple, and myrrh was an herb used for burial, a foreshadowing of Jesus' death.

- Have the children come prepared to give an offering: money, a toy, or a gift for someone in need. The money can be used to support one of the worthy ministries mentioned earlier or another of your choosing.

- Play one of the games introduced in the study, or another game that you enjoy.

- Host a White Elephant gift exchange. To do this, each child brings a wrapped, silly gift. The children are each given a number. Number one chooses his gift and unwraps it. Number two can either choose number one's gift or a new one. As soon as he chooses and unwraps his gift, number three chooses. He picks one of the first two gifts or a new one. Play goes on until all the children have a present. The only rule is that once a gift has changed hands three times, it can no longer be taken away. Another option is to exchange Christmas ornaments instead of silly gifts. Ornaments are usually on sale after Christmas, so you might want to get yours early if you choose this option.

- Recite memory verse(s).

- Sing "The Twelve Days of Christmas" in a round. Seat everyone in a circle, grouped so there are twelve groups. Assign each group a number, one through twelve. The first group leads out, singing, "On the first day of Christmas, my true love gave to me a partridge in a pear tree." Then the second group sings the second verse, with the first group coming in with "and a partridge in a pear tree." The third group sings the third verse, and group two sings "two turtle doves," group one sings "and a partridge in a pear tree", and so on until the song is finished. Each group can make their verse as silly or funny as they want. It is meant to be fun.

However you choose to celebrate, the Three Kings Cake (Appendix B) should be the centerpiece of the party. The child who finds the prize hidden in the middle of the cake is crowned king or queen for the day. Give this child the place of honor, robe them in purple, and give them a royal scepter. Do whatever you choose to make the child feel special. The children should all have an opportunity to share what they have learned, with the king or queen overseeing the proceedings. If possible, the children could have photos of their journey arranged in an album to show as they tell their story.

At the end of the party, the king or queen for the day should say a prayer of blessing for the rest of the year and declare the party finished. The prayer can be written beforehand, in case of a shy king or queen.

Keep in mind that this is your party. You know what your family will like. Keep it as simple and stress-free as possible. And remember to have fun.

— APPENDIX B —

SCROLLS FOR THE 12 GIFTS

(On The Following Page)

Gift 1

God gave us the first and best gift his son, Jesus Christ. Our first gift to Him should be ourselves. Dedicate your life to him afresh and ask Jesus to help you finish this year and start the next with him as our guide. Praise His Glory.

BRINGING IT HOME TO YOUR HEART

We suggest that if you have not done so, go through the memory verses listed in Appendix A. Choose the ones you think are appropriate for the ages and stages of your children, and begin memorizing them on the appropriate days. For today, copy the chosen verse in your journal and write your prayer of commitment for the upcoming year. Help younger children understand the meaning of commitment. Allow them to draw pictures of what it means to them and how they will respond.

BE HIS HANDS AND FEET

Take an afternoon trip to see how we can shelter those who cannot shelter themselves. Spread some of his joy by visiting a homeless shelter, a children's home, a nursing home, a hospital, or another place of your choosing. If the facilities allow it, bring along some goodies to share. These could be candy, home-baked cookies or just a song and a smile.

God gave to us a precious gift, the bible, as a love letter in the form of the Old and New Testaments. This is how we can know Him and His direction for our lives. Our gift to Him is to get to know Him through His very special book, the Bible.

BRINGING IT HOME TO YOUR HEART

Work on your memory verse by playing the Bounce Back game (Appendix A). If you do not know them, this year may be a good time to try to memorize the books of the Bible. An easy way to learn these is a song recorded by Wee Sing. Record in your journal why it is important to write God's Word on your heart. Play the Prophecy Matching Game or the Obedience Game, or conduct a Bible drill. Rules for the games are listed in Appendix A.

Listen to this beautiful white dove cooing.
http://www.youtube.com/watch?v=8q7Zz39RBak& NR=1

BE HIS HANDS AND FEET

Purchase or make a bird feeder (Appendix B). Give it to your pastor or someone who is influential in your spiritual growth. Attach a note of thanks for their faithful service to you. You could also begin a prayer journal to remind you to pray for others and keep a log of God's answers.

Gift 3

Since God gave us these three gifts, faith, hope and love, we should give them back to Him by having faith and hope in Him, and loving Him with our whole hearts. We should also give these gifts back to Him to use. Ask him to grow these qualities in your life so that you may be an example to others.

BRINGING IT HOME TO YOUR HEART

Look up the definitions of faith, hope, and love in a dictionary. Compare the information to what the Bible has to say about these three virtues. Look up verses in your concordance and definitions in a Bible dictionary, if you have one. Discuss and create your best definition for each. Write them in your journal, along with where the verses are found. You could also start a list of your favorite verses. Read 1 Corinthians 13 to gain a better understanding of today's key verse. Review books of the Bible and memory verse.

BE HIS HANDS AND FEET

God has given us the gifts of faith, hope, and love. Share these gifts by sending a card to someone who needs encouragement, like a shut-in, someone who has suffered loss, or a person struggling with illness. Also, consider supporting a child through a world help organization like Compassion International, World Vision, Samaritan's Purse, or another worthy group. The contact information for these groups is listed in Appendix C.

Gift 4

Take the time this year to read though the four gospels. Learn their stories and how they complement each other. Also note the differences. Understand that each writer had his own personality and saw Jesus in a different light. This gives us a deeper and richer account of His life. Just like when a report is given of a particular event, the more people who tell the story, the broader the perspective. Knowing and understanding God's Word is not only a gift to God, but also a gift he gives to us.

BRINGING IT HOME TO YOUR HEART

The gospels tell us Jesus' story. But what about your own? Your story is called your testimony. It is unique to you, because it is what God has done in your life as you've learned how to trust him. Begin to record your story in your journal by writing one thing that is special to you about Jesus—one way that he is unique to your needs. You could also find a verse in one of the four gospels that is special to you and record that, too. Don't forget to review your memory verse.

BE HIS HANDS AND FEET

Tell someone your story. It could be your mom or dad, brother or sister, or another trusted friend. The more you practice sharing your faith, the easier it becomes. Then you will be ready when God gives you the opportunity to share your story, and his, with others.

God has given us so much, including the Torah. The best way to show Him our gratitude is to hold these truths dear to our hearts, love His law, and try to be obedient to Him.

BRINGING IT HOME TO YOUR HEART

Copy "The Golden Rule" (appendix A) on a piece of construction paper, cardstock, or other decorative paper and in your journal. Decorate the pages however you choose. You might like to use markers, crayons, colored pencils or stickers.

Memorize "The Five Golden Rules of Obedience"(appendix A). You can also decorate it and hang it some place where you will see it often and be reminded of what you learned. Record them in your journal. If possible, visit a synagogue. Ask the Rabbi to show you the Torah. Many still have it written in the form of a large beautiful scroll. If you ask, the Rabbi might even read some for you in the original Hebrew language. Don't forget to review your memory verse or begin to learn a new one.

BE HIS HANDS AND FEET

Bake a golden Bundt cake (Appendix B) or five mini-Bundt cakes. Share them with a neighbor or a friend and tell them what you have learned about gold and God's precious laws. You could even share your cake with the Rabbi at the synagogue. Just make sure the ingredients are kosher.

Gift 6

God created this wonderful world for us in six days. On the seventh day He rested. According to Genesis 2:2-3, "By the seventh day God had finished the work He had been doing; so on the seventh day He rested from all his work. And God blessed the seventh day and made it holy, because on it He rested from all the work He had done." Since even God rested, it is good for us to rest, too. This year, commit to keep the Sabbath: to rest, reflect, and keep it holy.

BRINGING IT HOME TO YOUR HEART

Read the first chapter of Genesis to learn what God created on each day. Remember that he created it for us to enjoy and to bring beauty and fullness to our lives. Take time to write or draw a picture in your journal of your favorite thing that God created. Write God a thank-you note along with it.

At the end of today's lesson and also in Appendix C, we have included some *great* internet links for you and your family. We hope you will take some time to learn a little more about God and his creation through these resources and others mentioned through this book. We truly have an awesome, marvelous God who loves us very much.

BE HIS HANDS AND FEET

Talk with your family about how you can honor God by keeping the Sabbath. Discuss what that would mean. Remember that every family will be different; don't worry if your Sabbath day looks different than someone else's. Ask God what would honor him and work toward that. Decide together what activities you will allow, and how to rest. Also, decide how you will respond when events arise that you choose not to participate in. This should be done in advance so you can honor God and be respectful to others. Record these choices in your journal for easy reference. These choices will not only honor God, but will also bring blessings to your life and family as you learn to rest and play.

Gift 7

With Jesus as our Savior, we are gifted with spiritual gifts. Using them is our gift back to Him. Discover your gifts and commit yourself to use them for Him.

BRINGING IT HOME TO YOUR HEART

Take a spiritual gifts survey to discover your gifts. There are many surveys on the internet. You can search for one using the key words "spiritual gifts survey" or you can go directly to http://www.kodachrome.org/spiritgift/ and take their test. Commit to using your gifts more. Keep the results in your journal. Review your memory verses and books of the Bible.

BE HIS HANDS AND FEET

Let the Holy Spirit guide you to use your spiritual gifts to bless others this week. Here are just a few suggestions: Write a letter to a soldier to encourage him. Perhaps, as you can afford, you can send him some small gifts to remind him of home. Check Appendix C for ministries that can help you connect with soldiers serving our country overseas. You could also do chores or yard work for someone who is unable to do it themselves. Perhaps you might like to adopt a college student or senior citizen. Try to do something special for someone in your family. Do it secretly. Write in your journal how your recipients reacted and how it blessed both them and you.

Gift 8

God gave us Jesus, who exemplified the beatitudes. Choose to be like Jesus through the different phases of your life. Think about what it means to live out these attitudes. Choose to act instead of reacting in difficult situations.

BRINGING IT HOME TO YOUR HEART

Work on memorizing the beatitudes. Write in your journal a situation in which you can choose to live one or more of the beatitudes. Review your memory verses and add another as you are ready. At dinner tonight, have each person share three or more things they have been grateful for that day. Try making this a new daily tradition. In this way we change our focus from what we don't have to what we are blessed with.

BE HIS HANDS AND FEET

Write a note of encouragement to someone who has been imprisoned for his faith. Go to www.voiceofthemartyrs.com to write your letter. Pray for him or her. If you have a soup kitchen or facility that feeds the homeless, volunteer to help.

God gave us his Spirit so he could grow fruit in us. We can choose to let him live in and through us.

BRINGING IT HOME TO YOUR HEART

Work on your memory verses. If possible, visit a nursery to see how fruit grows. Ask the gardener about pruning and other measures he takes to produce abundant, healthy fruit. Try to draw a parallel in your own life. What do you need to do to produce good spiritual fruit? If you live near a vineyard, take a tour and see how grapevines are tended. Also, you can attend a live showing of *The Nutcracker* or rent the performance and watch it together as a family. Write in your journal which fruit or fruits you would like to see grow in your life. This is also the reason we put decorative fruit on our Christmas tree.

BE HIS HANDS AND FEET

Deliver a fruit basket or a bottle of sparkling grape juice to someone who needs to sense God's Spirit today. Write a note to someone in your church who helps with the music or dance ministry, thanking them for their hard work. These are just a few ways you can exhibit the fruit of the Spirit.

Gift 10

Our gift to Him today is to praise God for His wisdom in providing the Ten Commandments for our protection and freedom by cheerfully obeying them.

BRINGING IT HOME TO YOUR HEART

Write the Ten Commandments on a scroll (Appendix B). Memorize them and write them in your journal. Review your memory verses from previous days. Make a plaque for your doorpost with the Ten Commandments on it and hang it on your door. Find out which government buildings post the Ten Commandments in public. Visit one and pray for the people who work there to know the richness of God's laws and his love for them.

BE HIS HANDS AND FEET

Make a list of our government officials that you can pray for. Create a prayer journal to record your concerns for them and the results of those prayers. Write letters to your leaders and let them know you are praying for them.

Gift 11

God is always faithful to us. Like the eleven faithful disciples, we must choose to remain faithful to him. You can do this by committing to spend time with him on a regular basis. Use a devotional guide or a Bible reading plan and read every day, either by yourself or together with your family. Talk to Him, too.

BRINGING IT HOME TO YOUR HEART

Memorize the names of the twelve disciples. They are: 1) Simon Peter 2) Andrew 3) James 4) John 5) Philip 6) Bartholomew 7) Matthew 8) Thomas 9) James bar (son of) Alpheus 10) Simon the Zealot 11) Thaddaeus and 12) Judas Iscariot who betrayed Jesus. Write them in your journal. Learn something about the character of one or more of the disciples. Pantomime something about them and have a friend guess who you are. Review your other memory work, too.

BE HIS HANDS AND FEET

Jesus' disciples followed him wherever he went. They assisted him in his tasks and met the needs of those around them as Jesus healed the sick and loved the unlovely. Today, think of some way you can be like his disciples and meet a need of someone you know. Ask your mom if you could help her around the house, or do something without being asked. Play a game or read a book with a younger brother or sister. Begin to make a habit of doing an unexpected act of service every day. Then as a family you can each share your act of service for the day at dinner time. You could also take some of your unused toys or clothing to an agency where they can be given to those who will use them. Make or purchase items to give to someone in need. You don't have to do all these things at once, but begin to make a deliberate practice of being his disciple.

Gift 12

We have arrived at our final gift for our savior. But really, this is not the final gift, but just the beginning; a lifelong gift of praise and worship. The psalmist said it this way:

> Let the heavens be glad and the earth rejoice!
> Let the sea and everything in it shout his praise!
> Let the fields and their crops burst out with joy!
> Let the trees of the forest rustle with praise.

We need to believe; not just that He exists, but trust in all that He says, all that He is, and all that He does. We need to realize our need for Him as our savior, and accept His gift of grace to us. God wants to have a relationship with us. He gave His son for us and created an amazing world for us to live in. He gave us His word and his Holy Spirit to guide us on our way. Our gift to Him is to believe, worship, and follow Him now and throughout the rest of our lives.

BRINGING IT HOME TO YOUR HEART

Read the *Apostles' Creed* and discuss each point. In your journal, write each point in your own words. Review all your memory work and congratulate yourself for a job well done. Remember too, that the angels are rejoicing for you.

BE HIS HANDS AND FEET

Today is Epiphany, or Three Kings Day.

Make a Three Kings Cake and invite neighbors or friends over for a Three Kings Party. Be creative; share your journal and what you have learned with your friends. Celebrate all God has done for you in the past twelve days, and look forward to what he is going to accomplish in and through you in this new year. Be sure to send us an email that tells us how you liked this guide and what suggestions you may have. We look forward to hearing what God is doing in you.

A Partridge in a Pear Tree

The partridge: Jesus, who gave his life for us
The pear tree: The cross, the tree upon which he was crucified
My true love: God, the one who loves us enough to give us his only Son

For God so loved the world that he gave his one and only Son, that whoever believes in
him shall not perish but have eternal life. John 3:16

Two Turtle Doves

Two turtledoves: the Old and New Testaments of the Bible, which is God's love story to us. Jesus is the fulfillment of the Old Testament prophesies.

When the time of their purification according to the Law of Moses had been completed, Joseph and Mary took him to Jerusalem to present him to the Lord (as it is written in the Law of the Lord, "Every firstborn male is to be consecrated to the Lord"), and to offer a sacrifice in keeping with what is said in the Law of the Lord: "a pair of doves or two young pigeons." Luke 2:22-24

Three French Hens

The three French hens represent the three virtues of faith, hope, and love.

Now these three remain: faith, hope and love. But the greatest of these is love.
I Corinthians 13:13

Four Calling Birds

The four calling birds represent the four gospels: Matthew, Mark, Luke, and John, which tell us the good news of God sending Jesus to reconcile us to himself.

But these are written that you may believe that Jesus is the Christ, the Son of God, and that by believing you may have life in his name. John 20:31

Five Golden Rings

The five golden rings represent the five books of Moses, known as the Torah, which is the law: Genesis, Exodus, Leviticus, Numbers, and Deuteronomy.

The fear of the Lord is pure, enduring forever.
The ordinances of the Lord are sure and altogether righteous.
They are more precious than gold, than much pure gold;
they are sweeter than honey, than honey from the comb. Psalms 19:9–10

Six Geese-A-Laying

Six geese-a-laying: eggs represent new life, the new life created on the six days of creation.

In the beginning, God created the heavens and the earth. Genesis 1:1

Seven Swans-A-Swimming

The seven swans-a-swimming represent the seven gifts of the Holy Spirit: prophecy, ministry, teaching, exhortation, giving, leading, and compassion.

We have different gifts, according to the grace given us. If a man's gift is prophesying, let him use it in proportion to his faith. If it is serving, let him serve; if it is teaching, let him teach; if it is encouraging, let him encourage; if it is contributing to the needs of others, let him give generously; if it is leadership, let him govern diligently; if it is showing mercy, let him do it cheerfully. Romans 12:6-8

Eight Maids-a-Milking

The eight maids-a-milking represent the eight beatitudes as outlined in Matthew 5:8-10.

Blessed are the poor in spirit, for theirs is the kingdom of heaven. Blessed are those who mourn, for they will be comforted. Blessed are the meek, for they will inherit the earth. Blessed are those who hunger and thirst for righteousness, for they will be filled. Blessed are the merciful, for they will be shown mercy. Blessed are the pure in heart, for they will see God. Blessed are the peacemakers, for they will be called sons of God. Blessed are those who are persecuted because of righteousness, for theirs is the kingdom of heaven.
Matthew 5:3-10

Nine Ladies Dancing

nine fruits of the Holy Spirit: love, joy, peace, patience, kindness, goodness, faithful-
ness, gentleness, and self-control.

But the fruit of the Spirit is love, joy, peace, patience, kindness, goodness, faithfulness,
gentleness, and self-control. Against such things there is no law. Galatians 5:22-23

Ten Lords-a-Leaping

The ten lords-a-leaping represent the Ten Commandments.

*I am the Lord your God, You shall have no other gods before Me. *You shall not make for yourself an idol, you shall not worship them or serve them; for I, the Lord your God, am a jealous God. *You shall not take the name of the Lord your God in vain. *Remember the Sabbath day, to keep it holy. Six days you shall labor and do all your work. *Honor your father and your mother, that your days may be prolonged in the land which the Lord your God gives you. *You shall not murder. *You shall not commit adultery. *You shall not steal. *You shall not bear false witness against your neighbor. *You shall not covet anything that belongs to your neighbor. Exodus 20:2-17*

Eleven Pipers Piping

11 faithful disciples

These are the twelve he appointed: Simon (to whom he gave the name Peter) James son of Zebedee and his brother John (to them he gave the name Boanerges, which means Sons of Thunder); Andrew, Philip, Bartholomew, Matthew, Thomas, James bar Alphaeus, Thaddaeus, Simon the Zealot, and Judas Iscariot, who betrayed him.
Mark 3:16–19

Twelve Drummers Drumming

The twelve tenants of our faith as outlined in the Apostle's Creed.

Apostles Creed
1. I believe in God, the Father Almighty, creator of heaven and earth. 2. I believe in Jesus Christ, his only Son, our Lord. 3. He was conceived by the power of the Holy Spirit and born of the virgin Mary. 4. He suffered under Pontius Pilate, was crucified, died, and was Buried. He decended into the grave. 5. On the third day he rose again. He ascended into heaver, and is seated at the right hand of the Father. 6. He will come again to judge the living and the dead. 7. I believe in the Holy Spirit, 8. The Holy Church, 9. The communion of the saints, 10. the forgiveness of sins, 11. the resurrection of the body, 12. and life everlasting.

THE TWELVE DAYS OF CHRISTMAS

On the first day of Christmas my true love sent to me a partridge in a pear tree.

2-4. On the [second - fourth] day of Christmas my true love sent to me

Four calling birds, Three French Hens, Two turtle doves,
and a partridge in a pear tree.

5. On the fifth day of Christmas my true love sent to me Five golden rings!

5-12. Four calling birds, Three French Hens, Two turtle doves and a partridge in a pear tree.

6-12. On the [sixth - twelfth] day of Christmas my true love sent to me

Six geese a laying,
Seven swans a swimming,
Eight maids a milking,
Nine ladies dancing,
Ten lords a-leaping,
Eleven pipers piping,
Twelve drummers drumming,

BIRDFEEDER INSTRUCTIONS:

Birds will love these treats that can be made from easy-to-acquire materials.

BIRDFEEDER #1: AN EASY TREAT FOR YOUR FEATHERED FRIENDS

Materials:

> Large pinecones
> Peanut butter and/or honey (some birds prefer honey to peanut butter)
> Birdseed
> Plastic freezer bag or sandwich bag and string

Instructions:

Pour or spread the peanut butter, honey, or a mixture of both over the pinecone. The pinecone can also be dipped in the mixture. Place about two cups of birdseed and the pinecone in the zip-top bag. Shake it until the cone is covered in seed. Remove the cone and tie a string at the top. Hang it on a branch near a window so you can watch your friends enjoy their treats. If you are going to give this away as a gift, wrap it in plastic wrap or waxed paper and place it in a decorated paper bag. Don't forget to include instructions for hanging and a note of thanks.

BIRDFEEDER #2: THIS FEEDER ALSO MAKES A GREAT GIFT, AND THE SQUIRRELS WILL LOVE IT TOO.

Materials:

> Empty and washed plastic milk jug (gallon or half-gallon size)
> String
> Birdseed
> Twigs, small dowel, or bamboo skewers

Instructions:

Poke several tiny holes in the bottom of the milk jug to allow water to drain. Cut two small openings (about 1 to 2 inches square), one on either side of the jug, near the container's middle. Poke your skewers or twigs into the jug, (just below the opening you just cut), for perches. Tie a string around the handle for hanging. Decorate if you choose. Using a funnel, fill with seed just to the holes you cut. Put the lid on and enjoy.

BIRDFEEDER #3

This is very similar to #2, except a paper milk carton is used instead of a jug. Cut the openings to make them look like little doors. Then the carton can be painted to look like a house. To make a perch, poke a skewer or twig all the way through the carton, leaving a portion sticking out on either side. Place a string through the top for hanging. Fill the carton up to the holes with seed for your friends to enjoy.

Variations:

Little ones can string Cheerios or fruit-ring cereal on yarn to form rings. These can be hung on a tree branch for the birds to enjoy. Children can also string stale pieces of bread with thin apple slices and hang the strings in the tree. The internet offers instructions for many other feeders as well.

THE GOLDEN RULE

DO UNTO *Others* AS *You* WOULD HAVE THEM DO UNTO *You*

GOLDEN APPLE BUNDT CAKE

2 cups sugar
¼ cup orange juice
4 eggs
3 teaspoons baking powder
1 cup chopped nuts

1 cup oil
2 ½ teaspoons vanilla
3 cups flour
½ teaspoon salt

Filling:

2 cups chopped apples
1 tablespoon sugar
1 teaspoon ground cinnamon
Confectioner's sugar for dusting

In a small bowl, make the filling by mixing apples, 1 tablespoon sugar, and cinnamon. Set aside.

In a medium bowl, sift together flour, baking powder, and salt. In a large bowl, beat sugar, oil, eggs, orange juice, and vanilla. Add the flour mixture. Fold in nuts.

Pour a third of the batter into a greased Bundt or tube pan. Top with half of the filling. Then layer more batter, and then filling, then end with batter.

Bake in 350° oven for 55–60 minutes, or until top springs back when touched.

Remove cake from pan while it is still warm. Dust with confectioners' sugar and enjoy.

GOLDEN BUNDT CAKE

8 ounces cream cheese, softened
½ cup warm water
1 box yellow cake mix
2 tablespoons butter, melted
½ cup sugar
½ cup oil
4 eggs

Mix cream cheese and warm water together. Add cake mix, butter, and sugar to the cream cheese mixture. And eggs one at a time, mixing well after each. Pour batter into greased and floured Bundt pan. Bake at 325° for 35–45 minutes.

GOLDEN DELICIOUS BUNDT CAKE

3 Golden Delicious apples, peeled and diced
1 cup pecan pieces
½ cup sugar
2 teaspoons ground cinnamon
4 large eggs
2/3 cup safflower or canola oil
2¼ cups sugar
1 cup applesauce
1½ teaspoons vanilla extract
3 cups all-purpose flour
3½ teaspoons baking powder
½ teaspoon salt

Directions:

Heat oven to 350°. Grease and flour a twelve-cup Bundt pan. In a small mixing bowl, combine peeled and diced apples, pecan pieces, ½ cup of the sugar, and the cinnamon. Stir to blend; set aside. In a large mixing bowl, mix oil, sugar, applesauce, and vanilla. In another bowl, combine flour, baking powder, and salt. Slowly beat dry ingredients into the applesauce mixture until well blended. Stir in the diced apple mixture. Spoon into the prepared baking pan. Bake for 80–90 minutes or until a cake tester or wooden pick comes out with a few crumbs clinging. Cool in pan on a rack for 15 minutes. If necessary, loosen sides with a spatula. Put the rack over the pan and carefully invert. Cool completely. Slide the cooled cake onto a serving plate, or to be safe, place the baking pan over the cake again, flip with the rack, then cover with a serving plate and invert again.

THE FIVE GOLDEN RULES OF OBEDIENCE

LEARN THESE

OF OBEDIENCE

1. I WILL HAVE A JOYFUL HEART IN ALL I DO.

2. I WILL OBEY THOSE WHO ARE RESPONSIBLE FOR ME IMMEDIATELY BECAUSE DELAYED OBEDIENCE IS DISOBEDIENCE.

3. I WILL NOT HAVE A WHINING OR COMPLAINING SPIRIT.

4. I WILL OBEY FULLY AND COMPLETELY.

5. I WILL GO ABOVE AND BEYOND, GOING THE EXTRA MILE.

TABLE OF GIFTS

This is an interesting table that calculates how many gifts are received.
If you total up all the gifts, there is one for each day of the year!

One Gift for each day of the year	Day 1	Day 2	Day 3	Day 4	Day 5	Day 6	Day 7	Day 8	Day 9	Day 10	Day 11	Day 12	Total
Partridge in a pear tree	1	1	1	1	1	1	1	1	1	1	1	1	12
Turtle Doves		2	2	2	2	2	2	2	2	2	2	2	22
French Hens			3	3	3	3	3	3	3	3	3	3	30
Calling Birds				4	4	4	4	4	4	4	4	4	36
Gold Rings					5	5	5	5	5	5	5	5	40
Geese-a-Laying						6	6	6	6	6	6	6	42
Swans-a-Swimming							7	7	7	7	7	7	42
Maids-a-Milking								8	8	8	8	8	40
Ladies Dancing									9	9	9	9	36
Lords-a-Leaping										10	10	10	30
Pipers Pipping											11	11	22
Drummers Drumming												12	12
Total	1	3	6	10	15	21	28	36	45	55	66	78	364

INSTRUCTIONS FOR TEN COMMANDMENTS SCROLL AND PLAQUE

You can simply copy the simple version of the Ten Commandments in Appendix A and frame it or you can create your own.

Scroll Materials: one 8½ x 11 inch paper; two straws, sticks, or bamboo skewers with the points cut off; tape; a length of ribbon

Have your children print (via handwriting or on the computer) the Ten Commandments onto the piece of paper. The paper should be landscape oriented, with the long lengths of the paper at top and bottom, short lengths on the side. Decorate; one idea is to make it look old by crumpling it or dyeing it with tea. Tape the straws to the short sides of the paper and roll the paper around the straws, both at the same time, toward the middle. Use a ribbon to tie your scroll.

To make the plaque, you will need a piece of wood, at least six inches square, any shape. If you have a knack for woodworking, you can cut the wood in the shape of the stone tablets that God gave to Moses. If you choose to cut the wood yourself, don't forget to sand it afterwards. Affix the Ten Commandments to your plaque however you choose, by painting them, printing them off and decoupaging them, burning with a wood burner, etc. Decorate it with any desired materials. Cover it with decoupage glue, stain, and/or shellac. Place a wall hook on the back and hang.

THE TEN COMMANDMENTS
Exodus 20

I am the Lord your God, You shall have no other gods before Me.

You shall not make for yourself an idol, you shall not worship them or serve them; for I, the Lord your God, am a jealous God.

You shall not take the name of the Lord your God in vain.

Remember the Sabbath day, to keep it holy. Six days you shall labor and do all your work.

Honor your father and your mother, that your days may be prolonged in the land which the Lord your God gives you.

You shall not murder.

You shall not commit adultery.

You shall not steal.

You shall not bear false witness against your neighbor.

You shall not covet anything that belongs to your neighbor.

THE TEN COMMANDMENTS

Then God spoke all these words, saying,

I am the Lord your God, who brought you out of the land of Egypt, out of the house of slavery.

You shall have no other gods before me.

You shall not make for yourself an idol, or any likeness of what is in heaven above or on the earth beneath or in the water under the earth.

You shall not worship them or serve them; for I, the Lord your God, am a jealous God, visiting the iniquity of the fathers on the children, on the third and the fourth generations of those who hate me, but showing loving kindness to thousands, to those who love me and keep my commandments.

You shall not take the name of the Lord your God in vain, for the Lord will not leave him unpunished who takes his name in vain.

Remember the Sabbath day, to keep it holy.

Six days you shall labor and do all your work, but the seventh day is a Sabbath of the Lord your God; in it you shall not do any work, you or your son or your daughter, your male or your female servant or your cattle or your sojourner who stays with you.

For in six days the Lord made the heavens and the earth, the sea and all that is in them, and rested on the seventh day; therefore the Lord blessed the Sabbath day and made it holy.

Honor your father and your mother, that your days may be prolonged in the land which the Lord your God gives you.

You shall not murder.

You shall not commit adultery.

You shall not steal.

You shall not bear false witness against your neighbor.

You shall not covet your neighbor's house; you shall not covet your neighbor's wife or his male servant or his female servant or his ox or his donkey or anything that belongs to your neighbor.

The Ten Commandments (Simplified Version)
Exodus 20

I am the LORD your God, You shall have no other gods before Me.

You shall not make for yourself an idol, you shall not worship them or serve them; for I, the LORD your God, am a jealous God.

You shall not take the name of the LORD your God in vain.

Remember the Sabbath day, to keep it holy. Six days you shall labor and do all your work.

Honor your father and your mother, that your days may be prolonged in the land which the LORD your God gives you.

You shall not murder.

You shall not commit adultery.

You shall not steal.

You shall not bear false witness against your neighbor.

You shall not covet anything that belongs to your neighbor.

All the people perceived the thunder and the lightning flashes and the sound of the trumpet and the mountain smoking; and when the people saw it, they trembled and stood at a distance. (Exodus 20)

Note: in each of the following recipes, it is suggested that you bake a bean, almond, or small figurine (not plastic) into your cake. As an easy alternative, you can place your bean, almond or figurine on your cake plate before you invert your cake onto it. Then gently poke it in the cake from the under side with your finger. Be sure to let the children know to be careful and look for the item before they dig in!

GERMAN THREE KING'S CAKE (DREIKÖNIGSKUCHEN)

2 cups flour
1 package yeast
1/3 cup sugar
¼ cup butter or margarine, melted
Small figurine, almond, or dried bean

½ teaspoon salt
1 finely chopped whole lemon, seeds removed
½ teaspoon cardamom
2 eggs, 1 separated
½ cup raisins, soaked in warm apple juice

Frosting
2 tablespoons powdered sugar
2 tablespoons lemon juice
½ cup red candied cherries, halved

Directions

Place the flour in a large bowl. Make a hole in the middle of the flour, put the yeast into it and mix together with the flour, sugar and the milk. Cover with a cloth and let rise in a warm place for 15 minutes. Add the melted butter, salt, lemon, cardamom, egg, egg white, and flour and yeast mixture. Knead dough until smooth. When the dough begins to form a ball, stir in raisins and fruit. Form dough into a log. Cut off a quarter of the log; divide the quarter into four equal parts, and form balls from each. Divide the remaining log into four parts and form balls from each. Poke the bean, almond or figurine into the dough. Grease well a spring form pan with a central tube. Place dough into the pan, alternating large and small dough balls. Cover the pan and let rise in a warm place until doubled. Brush the dough with the beaten yolk and place in a pre-heated, 350° oven for approximately 30 minutes. Cool cake thoroughly before removing from pan. Mix the powdered sugar with lemon juice to an icing consistency (not too liquid). Ice the cake, and decorate with the candied cherries. In Germany, a small gold crown made of foil is placed in the middle of the cake after frosting. Slice and serve.

FRENCH KING'S CAKE (GALETTE DES ROIS)

9-ounce puff pastry
½ cup butter, melted
1 egg yolk mixed with a drop or two of water
Almond paste
A small dry bean

Directions:

Preheat oven to 350°.

Divide the puff pastry in half. Unroll and trim to form two discs. Place the first disc on a baking sheet and spread a layer of almond paste on top. Place the bean somewhere on the almond paste, which will cause it to be baked inside the pastry. Cover with the second circle of pastry. If you would like, you can cut shapes into the top few layers of pastry with cookie cutters or a knife to create a decorative pattern. Brush the top with the beaten egg yolk mixture. Bake at 350° for 15–20 minutes or until nicely browned. To serve, slice like a pie with a sharp knife. Whoever gets the bean is the king or queen for the day.

SPANISH EPIPHANY BREAD

3 cups white flour
1/3 cup butter
1/3 cup sugar
1 ounce yeast dissolved in ½ cup warm water
2 teaspoons lemon zest
2 teaspoons orange zest
1 tablespoon brandy
2 eggs + 1 egg white, well beaten
1 tablespoon orange flower water
A pinch of salt
1 silver coin, china figurine, dry bean, or whole almond
Large pieces of candied fruit
Flaked almonds

Directions:

Place the flour and salt into a large bowl and mix together with your hands. Make a well in the center of the flour mixture and pour in the dissolved yeast mixture. Gradually mix in the rest of the flour. Cover with a towel and let rest for 15 minutes. In the meantime, cream the butter and sugar together. Mix the zests, brandy, orange-flower water, and the two eggs into the dough. Knead until it becomes smooth. Gradually mix in the butter, kneading constantly, until the dough becomes smoother and more elastic. Cover and let rise in a warm place for about 90 minutes, until the dough has doubled in volume. Turn dough out onto a floured surface and knead for 2–3 minutes. Add the silver coin, figurine, bean, or almond. Roll the dough into a long, sausage shape, approximately 2 feet long and 5 inches thick. Place on a baking sheet and form into a ring. Pinch the ends together. Cover with a damp towel and let rest another 30–45 minutes or until the dough has doubled in size again. Preheat oven to 350°. Brush the dough with the beaten egg white and decorate with the almonds and slices of candied fruit, pressing them down so that they stick to the dough. Place into a 350° oven and bake for 30–35 minutes until the bread is cooked and golden brown. When done, remove from the pan, place on a rack, and let cool. When you serve, the person who gets the coin, figurine, bean, or almond is the king or queen for the day.

MEXICAN KING'S CAKE (LA ROSCA DE REYES)

½ tablespoon active dry yeast
2 tablespoons warm water (105–115°)
1/3 cup milk
3 tablespoons sugar
¼ teaspoon salt
3 tablespoons unsalted butter
2½ cups flour
1 egg
2 tablespoons golden raisins
1 tablespoon chopped nuts or blanched almonds
1 tablespoon sugar
2 tablespoons chopped mixed candied fruit (e.g. figs, oranges, cherries, citrons),
     plus extra for decoration
1 baby figurine

Glaze
1 egg, beaten with 1 tablespoon water

Directions

Dissolve yeast in warm water and set aside for 5 minutes. Heat milk, sugar, salt, and butter until warm (105–115°). In a large bowl, combine yeast mixture, milk mixture, 1½ cups flour, and egg. Mix thoroughly. Add enough remaining flour to form a soft dough. Knead on lightly floured surface or in an electric mixer for about 10 minutes. Place in greased bowl, turning to coat top. Cover and let rise in a warm place until it doubles in size, about one hour. Lightly knead in raisins, candied fruit, and nuts. Return to the greased bowl, turning to coat top. Cover and let rise in a warm place until it doubles in size, about 45 minutes. Punch down dough and insert the baby figurine. Shape into a round loaf. Make a 4" hole in center and shape dough into a ring ("rosca") about eight inches across. Place on greased baking sheet. Butter the outside of a 3 or 4-inch custard dish and set it in the hole. Cover and let bread rise in warm place for 30 minutes. Preheat the oven to 350°. Brush egg glaze on loaf. Press whole candied fruits and nuts on top and sprinkle with sugar. Bake at 350° for 25–30 minutes or until golden. Remove to a wire rack to cool. Slice and serve. The person who gets the token is the king or queen for the day.

Glaze Alternative

> After loaves are cooled, mix the following ingredients until fluffy and well blended:
> 3 cups powdered sugar
> 6 tablespoons butter
> 2 tablespoons milk
> 2 tablespoons vanilla
> Spread over cooled loaf and decorate with multi-colored sugars or candied fruit.

AMERICAN EASY THREE KINGS CAKE
(not traditional, but fun!)

> Frozen or homemade bread dough (sweet bread preferred, but not essential)
> Candied or dried fruit, raisins, or mini candy-coated chocolates
> 1 teaspoon cinnamon mixed with ½ cup sugar
> 1 dry bean

> *Glaze*
> 1 cup confectioners' sugar and several tablespoons of milk

Directions

If using frozen dough, thaw until workable. Roll out dough on a lightly floured or oiled surface until about ¾ inch thick. Sprinkle with cinnamon-sugar mixture. Roll up jelly-roll style and knead into a ball again. Roll out to a 14 inch rectangle and sprinkle with fruit, raisins, or candies. Roll up again and place the entire roll on a greased pan on which you will form and bake your "crown." Slice at ½ inch intervals only three fourths of the way through the dough. Try to make an even number of slices, which would require an odd number of cuts. Insert the bean into one of the slices. The next part is a little tricky to describe. Basically, you are alternate slices to the left and then to the right, forming the whole thing into the shape of a ring or crown. Take the first and pull slightly, twist and lay flat to the left on the tray. Then take the next slice, pull slightly and lay flat to the right. Continue with all the slices, and as you alternate, also shape the entire log into a ring so that your first slice and your last slice slightly overlap. Hopefully they will be opposite. If not, fudge a bit and leave it toward the middle. Brush with melted butter and let rise for about 30 minutes or until doubled. Bake in a 350° oven for 20–30 minutes or until golden and hollow-sounding. Cool. Make glaze by mixing powdered sugar with milk, one tablespoon at a time until easy to spread. Drizzle or spread the glaze over the crown. Pull apart to eat. The person who gets the bean is the queen or king for the day.

Another fun way to shape the dough is to roll it out after you add the fruit, into the shape of a pizza. Place it on a pizza pan and put a cup or glass, about 2 to 3 inches in diameter, in the center. Press down slightly to make an indentation, but do not cut all the way through. With a pair of kitchen shears, cut from the edge of the dough to the center indentation in strips about 1 inch wide. Twist each strip and push the bean into one of the strips. Then brush the entire ring with melted butter. Let rise and bake as directed above. Cool and drizzle with glaze.

Be sure to check our website www.12daysbook.com for photographs of these cakes and other recipes that we use to make our celebration more special.

Websites for writing to soldiers and veterans:

> www.forgottensoldiers.org
> www.soldiersangels.org
> www.americasupportsyou.mil

Website for writing to Christians who are imprisoned for their faith:

> The Voice of the Martyrs
> www.persecution.com

Websites for World Relief Organizations:

> www.compassion.com
> www.worldvision.org
> www.samaritanspurse.org

Website to access your government officials:

> www.congress.org

Coloring pages

> http://www.kidsturncentral.com/coloring/12dayscolor.htm

Link for day two

> http://www.youtube.com/watch?v=8q7Zz39RBak&NR=1

Links for day six

> These three short videos are well worth watching. Even my older children enjoyed them.
>
> http://www.kids4truth.com/eng_creation.htm
> http://www.kids4truth.com/watchmaker/watch.html
> http://www.kids4truth.com/cv/voice.html

Excellent video on evolution by Kirk Cameron for you and your older children

> http://www.wayofthemaster.com/evolution.shtml

http://www.jonathanpark.com/ An excellent audio drama series that is creation science based, similar to *Adventures in Odyssey,* and great for car trips. They also have great resources and activities for kids on their web site.

http://www.apologiaonline.com/conf/ Apologia Educational Ministries Inc. Click on the title of any of the conference handouts to read them.